Tragic Prelude:

BLEEDING KANSAS

Linnet Books by Karen Zeinert

The Lincoln Murder Plot (1999)

The Amistad Slave Revolt and American Abolition (1997)

Across the Plains in the Donner Pary by Virginia Reed Murphy (1996)

Captured by Indians: The Life of Mary Jemison (1995)

*Memoirs of Andrew Sherburne: Patriot and Privateer of
the American Revolution* (1993)

Tragic Prelude:
BLEEDING KANSAS

BY KAREN ZEINERT

Linnet Books
North Haven, Connecticut

Library of Congress Cataloging-in-Publication Data
Zeinert, Karen.
  Tragic prelude : bleeding Kansas / by Karen Zeinert.
    p. cm.
  Includes bibiographical references and index.
  ISBN 0-208-02446-8 (lib. bdg. : alk. paper)
    1. Kansas—Politics and government—1854-1861—Juvenile literature.
2. Antislavery movements—Kansas—History—19th century—Juvenile literature. 3. Slavery—Political aspects—Kansas—History—19th century—Juvenile
literature. 4. Violence—Kansas—History—19th century—Juvenile literature.
5. United States—History—Civil War, 1861-1865—Causes—Juvenile literature. [1. Kansas—History—Sources. 2. Slavery—Sources. 3. United States—
History—Civil War, 1861-1865—Causes—Sources.] I. Title.

F685 .Z45 2001
978.1'02—dc21   00-069435

The paper in this publication meets the minimum requirements of
American National Standard for Information Sciences—
Permanence of Paper for Printed Library Materials,
ANSI Z39.48—1984. ∞

Designed by Carol Sawyer of Rose Design

Printed in the United States of America

To Dr. Anthony W. Phillips
with deepest gratitude

BLEEDING KANSAS

KANSAS   MISSOURI

Atchinson •

Missouri River

Kickapoo •
Ft. Leavenworth •

Pawnee •   *Kansas River*   Topeka   Lecompton   Wyandotte •   • Westport
• Ft. Riley   Ft. Titus •   • Lawrence
                        Wakarusa River Big Springs • Franklin •   Shawnee
                                   Ft. Saunders •   • Prairie City   Mission

Marais des Cygnes River

• Pottawatomie Creek

Ft. Scott • •

NEBRASKA TERR.
Missouri
River
KANSAS TERR.

Kansas and Nebraska Territories in 1854–1861

vi

Contents

Introduction

In 1854, the U.S. Congress created Kansas Territory. Whether the state that would follow would allow slavery within its borders was up to the territory's citizens. So some Northerners, determined at all costs to stop the spread of slavery, and their opponents in the South, equally determined to gain yet another slave state, began to dream about finding some way to influence the settlers to make Kansas into what they thought it should be. Other Northern and Southern sympathizers, more than ten thousand strong, took more direct action: they rushed into the territory to claim it for their side.

The settlers' long-held beliefs ran deep, and as the two sides sparred for control, violent incidents, some of which were downright shocking, became commonplace. In fact, more than two hundred people lost their lives before federal troops finally intervened in the area, which because of the bloodshed there, became known as "Bleeding Kansas."

The struggle over slavery in the territory, a story chock-full of villains, heroes, and incredible plots, was a significant event in American history for several reasons. First and foremost, the conflict spread far beyond the borders of Kansas, deepening the divisions over slavery in America, tearing apart one political party, and giving rise to another.

This struggle also served as a dire warning and a dramatic foreshadowing of the catastrophe that would befall the country in only a few years. In fact, events in Bleeding Kansas were nothing less than a tragic prelude to America's bloodiest confrontation, the Civil War.

Cast of Characters

ATCHISON, DAVID — Proslavery senator from Missouri; former acting vice president of the United States; one of the leaders of the border ruffians

BROWN, JOHN — Abolitionist; leader of the Pottawatomie Creek massacres

DOUGLAS, STEPHEN A. — Senator from Illinois; author of the Kansas-Nebraska Act

GEARY, JOHN — Third governor of Kansas Territory

JONES, SAMUEL — Proslavery supporter; sheriff; leader of the posse that invaded Lawrence

LANE, JAMES — Leader of Free State forces; military commander for Committee of Safety in Lawrence; organized Army of the North; senator from Kansas

LECOMPTE, SAMUEL — Chief justice of the territorial supreme court; a slaveholder

MONTGOMERY, JAMES — Leader of antislavery militia in southeast Kansas Territory; a Jayhawker

PIERCE, FRANKLIN — President of the United States from 1853 to 1857

REEDER, ANDREW — First governor of Kansas Territory; joined Free Staters when fired as governor; leader of Free State forces

ROBINSON, CHARLES — Agent for New England Emigrant Aid Society in Kansas; leader of Free State forces; first governor of the state of Kansas

ROBINSON, SARA — Wife of Charles Robinson; published book about life in Kansas Territory; a Free Stater

ROPES, HANNAH — Settler in Kansas Territory; published a book about her experiences in Kansas Territory; a free soiler

SHANNON, WILSON — Second governor of Kansas Territory

STRINGFELLOW, JOHN — Editor of the proslavery newspaper, the *Squatter Sovereign*; a leader of the border ruffians

SUMNER, CHARLES — Abolitionist; a senator from Massachusetts; attacked for his speech titled "The Crime Against Kansas"

SUMNER, E.V. — Military leader at Fort Leavenworth

WALKER, ROBERT — Fourth governor of Kansas Territory

WHITFIELD, J.W. — Proslavery supporter; elected as territorial representative to U.S. Congress; a member of the border ruffians

Timeline

1854   ★ The Kansas-Nebraska Act is passed on May 22.

       ★ The first settlers arrive in Kansas Territory on June 10.

       ★ The first emigrant colony bound for Kansas leaves Boston on July 17.

       ★ The first election (for territorial delegate) in Kansas is held on November 29.

1855   ★ Settlers vote for members of the territorial legislature on March 30. Missourians stuff the ballot boxes. The results are declared null and void, and another election is held on May 22.

       ★ First territorial legislators, all proslavery, meet in July.

       ★ Free-soil supporters and abolitionists meet in July and August. They start the Free State party.

       ★ Free Staters meet at Big Springs on September 5. Members decide to form their own government.

       ★ Free Staters hold constitutional convention on October 23.

       ★ Proslavery forces start Law and Order party on November 14. They are determined to stop the Free State movement.

       ★ Charles Dow is murdered on November 21.

       ★ Jacob Branson is rescued by Lawrencians on November 27, putting Lawrence in jeopardy.

       ★ Border Army prepares to invade Lawrence on December 5. Before forces do so, a truce is agreed upon.

       ★ Free Staters vote on a constitution on December 15.

1856   ★ Free Staters elect officers in January. They decide to send James Lane to Washington in March. He applies for statehood for Kansas.

       ★ U.S. Representatives have many questions about statehood. They send three members to the territory to gather information. The men arrive in Kansas in April.

       ★ Federal troops arrive in Lawrence on April 21 to arrest Free Staters involved in Jacob Branson's rescue.

       ★ Sheriff Jones is shot on April 23.

       ★ Free State leaders are charged with treason on May 5, and warrants for their arrest are sworn out.

★ Senator Charles Sumner gives his famous "Crime Against Kansas" speech on May 20. He is attacked by Preston Brooks two days later.

★ Lawrence is invaded on May 21.

★ John Brown and his supporters massacre five proslavery settlers near Pottawatomie Creek on May 24 and 25 to retaliate for the invasion of Lawrence.

★ A reign of terror begins in June.

★ James Lane and his Army of the North arrive in Kansas in August.

★ James Lane and John Brown take three proslavery strongholds in mid-August.

★ Governor Geary takes over in September. He restores peace.

★ Presidential elections are held in November. The Democratic nominee, James Buchanan, wins by a narrow margin.

1857 ★ Fighting resumes in the territory in the spring, especially in the southeast, where Jayhawkers are active.

★ Governor Geary resigns. Robert Walker takes over in May.

★ Free Staters run candidates and vote in fall elections. They win a majority of seats in the territorial legislature.

★ The Lecompton Constitution is drafted in the fall by proslavery delegates.

1858 ★ Free Staters force a vote on the Lecompton Constitution in January. The document is rejected. President Buchanan asks Congress to admit Kansas to the Union under this constitution anyway. Congress refuses to do so.

★ Proslavery forces slaughter five Free Staters near the Marais des Cygnes River on May 19. It is the last major violent confrontation over slavery in the territory.

★ A constitutional convention is held in Wyandotte in July. This constitution is approved by voters in October. Kansans apply for statehood shortly after. Their application meets stiff resistance from Southerners.

1861 ★ Kansas is granted statehood on January 29.

★ Abraham Lincoln is inaugurated President of the United States on March 4.

★ Confederate forces fire on Fort Sumter; the Civil War begins on April 12.

Chapter One
A Shocking Attack

Early in the morning on May 23, 1856, in a small cabin in what is now eastern Kansas, abolitionist John Brown made his decision: his enemies' blood had to be spilled, and spilled in such a way as to shock and terrify all slaveholders in the area. Such an attack, Brown believed, would not only punish some of his adversaries for a recent assault, it would force others to flee for their lives, ending their attempts to make Kansas into a slave territory.

John Brown, one of American history's most unusual—and controversial—figures, had failed at almost every venture he had tried so far—running a tannery, speculating in land, or acting as a wool merchant. As a result, he had spent most of his life in poverty. Deeply devoted to the abolition of slavery, Brown, along with Oliver, one of eighteen children he had fathered, had moved to Kansas after receiving word from several of his sons who had recently settled there that Brown's help was needed to make Kansas a free state.

Brown had long believed that God had chosen him for a special mission, and now in the early hours of May 23, he thought that he knew what it was. He began to fulfill his

This picture of John Brown was taken in the 1850s. It is part of the Brady-Handy Collection and may have been taken by the now famous Mathew Brady, who recorded the Civil War for posterity. Courtesy of the Library of Congress

assumed calling by lining up eight men who were willing to do his bidding: five of his sons, Fred, Salmon, Owen, Watson, and Oliver; his son-in-law, Henry Thompson; and two of his neighbors, James Townsley and Theodore Weiner. These men eagerly gathered their rifles, knives, and sabers and piled them high in a large wagon. Then all except Weiner, who rode his own horse, clambered aboard behind their leader.

This group was bound for a not-too-distant ravine where the Mosquito and Pottawatomie creeks converged and numerous proslavery men and women had settled. After reaching their destination that afternoon, the men set up a temporary camp. When firewood had been secured, the horses bedded down, and guard duty decided upon, the men began to hone their sabers to razor-edge sharpness. While they did so, Brown, who had so far kept the details of his plan to himself, read a long list of victims who were to be killed, then described in graphic detail how they were going to die.

As Brown talked, neighbor James Townsley began to have second thoughts. Townsley didn't believe that Brown's plan would help their cause at all, arguing that such violence would only make their enemies even more determined and, worse yet, it might even turn some abolitionists against them. The two men argued most of that evening and a good part of the following day. Even after Brown agreed to limit the number of victims to six, Townsley balked. Brown, who had spent a lot of time praying before deciding upon his course of action, then played his trump card: This was a divine decision. "I have no choice," Brown said. "It has been decreed by Almighty God, ordained from eternity, that I should make an example of these men."[1]

Unable to dismiss Brown's most powerful argument, Townsley decided to try to get out of the attack by claiming that he was sick. Brown sneered at his neighbor and replied that all he needed was the sight and smell of blood to cure his ills. Outmaneuvered, Townsley halfheartedly accepted his leader's plan.

Late that evening, while Brown's proslavery targets were in bed and the attackers had the cover of night to protect them, the abolitionists left the ravine, crossed Mosquito Creek, and zeroed in on their first victims at James Doyle's farm. When all nine men had arrived at this homestead, around 11:00 p.m., they pounded on the cabin door and told Mr. Doyle and two of his adult sons, William and Drury, that they were under arrest. The prisoners were taken a short distance from the house, where they were killed.

Next Brown and his followers went to Allen Wilkinson's home. The men took Wilkinson from his cabin despite pleas from his sick wife that she needed his help. Although Brown told Mrs. Wilkinson that her husband was being taken to their camp, Brown's sons attacked and killed their prisoner less than one hundred yards from his home.

Eyewitness Account

Mrs. Allen Wilkinson gave a detailed account of what happened at the Wilkinson cabin on the night of May 24 to local officials. Her testimony was used to swear out a warrant for the arrest of John Brown and his supporters. She said:

> We were disturbed by [the] barking of the dog. I was sick
> with the measles, and woke up Mr. Wilkinson, and asked
> if he "heard the noise, and what it meant?" He said it was
> only some one passing about, and soon after was again
> asleep. It was not long before the dog raged and barked
> furiously, awakening me once more; pretty soon I heard
> footsteps as of men approaching; some one passed by the
> window, and some one knocked at the door. I asked,
> "Who is that?' Some one replied, "I want you to tell me
> the way to Dutch Henry's." [My husband] commenced to
> tell them, and they said to him, "Come out and show us."
> He wanted to go, but I would not let him; he then told
> them it was difficult to find his clothes, and could tell
> them as well without going out of doors. The men out of
> doors, after that, stepped back, and I thought I could hear
> them whispering; but they immediately returned, and as
> they approached, one of them asked my husband, "Are
> you . . . opposed to the Northern or free soil [antislavery]
> party [?]"

When my husband said, "I am," one of them said, "You are our prisoner. Do you surrender?" He said, "Gentlemen, I do." They said, "Open the door. . . .If you don't open it, we will open it for you." He opened the door against my wishes, and four men came in, and my husband was told to put on his clothes. . . . I begged them to let Mr. Wilkinson stay with me, saying that I was sick and helpless, and could not stay by myself. My husband also asked them to let him stay with me until he could get some one to wait on me; told them that he would not run off, but would be there the next day, or whenever called for. [Brown] . . . replied, "You have neighbors." I said, "So I have, but they are not here and I cannot go for them." [Brown] replied, "It matters not," and told [my husband] to get ready. He wanted to put on his boots . . . so as to be protected from the damp and night air, but they wouldn't let him. They then took [him] away. One of them came back and took two saddles; I asked him what they were going to do with [my husband], and he said, "Take him a prisoner to the camp. . . ."

After they were gone, I thought I heard my husband's voice. . . . [I] went to the door, and all was still.[2]

The last victims lived in James Harris's cabin, where Brown and his followers arrived about 2:00 a.m. on May 25. Harris somehow convinced the abolitionists that he should be spared, but William Sherman, who was staying with Harris, was not so lucky. Like the other victims, Sherman was marched out of the house at gunpoint and slaughtered. Brown and his men then rode off, leaving stunned survivors in three households to deal with the aftermath.

And what they found horrified them. Mr. Doyle had been shot in the head and stabbed through the heart. William and Drury Doyle had repeatedly been stabbed, and their skulls had been smashed open. In addition, Drury's arms had been severed from his body and his fingers had been hacked into bloody bits. Allen Wilkinson had been repeatedly attacked with sabers, as had William Sherman, whose brain lay exposed on the ground.

Word about the attacks spread quickly, and shortly after, many proslavery settlers—but to Brown's chagrin, not all—abandoned the Pottawatomie Creek area. Those who stayed, determined to hold on to their land at all costs, were especially cautious. One proslavery man said, "I never lie down without taking the precaution to fasten my door, and fix it in such a way that if it is forced open, it can be opened only wide enough for one person to come in at a time. I have my rifle, revolver, and . . . pistol where I can lay my hand on them in an instant, besides a hatchet & axe."[3]

Enraged by the attacks, more than a few slaveholders sought revenge. "Let us retaliate in the same manner," wrote one editor. "Let not the knives of the Pro-slavery men be sheathed while there is one Abolitionist in the Territory. As they have shown no quarter to our men, they deserve none from us. Let our motto be written in blood upon our flags, '*Death to all Yankees and traitors in Kansas!*'"[4]

Shortly after this announcement was made, numerous antislavery settlers fled the area.

The Pottawatomie Creek massacres were not the first reports of violence in the territory, although, to date, none had been so gruesome. Now as word about the attacks spread eastward, stunned Americans wondered aloud about what was happening in Kansas. After all, slavery had been a bitterly contested issue in many places for many years, and yet such blood-chilling events as the massacres at Pottawatomie Creek had not taken place. What then, made Kansas different? What indeed?

Chapter Two

SLAVE OR FREE?

B y the time settlers began to arrive in Kansas Territory in 1854, the fight over slavery in America was more than two hundred years old. In fact, the debate about whether Americans should own slaves began shortly after the first captives arrived in 1619 in what is now Virginia.

The issue continued to divide the country in the following years, and as a result, it was a hotly debated topic when the Constitutional Convention met in 1787 to set up a new government. How, antislavery delegates asked, could Americans have fought in a revolution for freedom and then deny freedom to others? But Southern delegates insisted upon keeping their slaves, some of whom were valued at more than $1,000 each.

In order to hold the delegates—and the country— together, the Convention sidestepped the issue by turning it back to the states, allowing them to decide for themselves whether or not to permit slavery within their borders. Also, to further pacify the South, delegates agreed to add three-fifths of each state's slave population to its total number of citizens before determining the number of delegates that state should have in the U. S. House of Representatives.

(However, even though slaves were counted for voting purposes, they could not cast a ballot.) As a result, the South gained an additional twenty representatives it would not have had without slaves, giving the Southern block in Congress considerable clout and angering many Northerners, especially those opposed to slavery.

Although many Americans had questioned the practice of slavery for years, it wasn't until the 1820s that the abolitionist movement began to gather steam. At that time, a spirit of change swept over America. Public-minded reformers tried to make the United States a better place for all, and they developed an impressive program. They wanted more educational opportunities for young people, more rights for women, better treatment for the mentally ill, and more help for the poor.

At the same time, a Christian revival swept over the country. It was part of what was known as the "Great Awakening." More people attended church than ever before, and day-long worship services drew people from near and far. Church leaders urged the faithful to reform America by fighting sin with all their might to create a great Christian nation that would truly please God.

Abolitionists employed the spirit of reform and religious zeal of the day to further their cause. They argued that slavery, besides being a grievous sin, was one of the sources of hatred and violence in American society. Therefore, until slavery was abolished, society could never really be improved, let alone be pleasing in God's sight. Abolitionists then asked for the support of all reformers.

But many reformers—as well as many other Americans—were reluctant to back the abolitionists for at least three reasons. First, the labor that slaves provided was important to the entire American economy. For example, the cotton that slaves produced not only made money for plantation owners, it was the major fiber used in Northern textile mills. Second, many Northerners and poor whites in the South were afraid that if the slaves were freed, they would take jobs away from white workers because the former slaves would be willing to work for lower wages. This would result in great economic hardship for many. And third, Americans resisted freeing the slaves because of racial prejudice. For years, Americans, and especially slaveowners, had convinced themselves that blacks were less than human in order to justify enslaving them.

Abolitionists, deeply upset by the public's lack of support for ending slavery in the early 1800s, were even more distraught when they were unable to prevent the spread of slavery into new territories. In 1804, the United States bought the Louisiana Purchase, more than 800,000 square miles of territory west of the Mississippi River, from France. In 1819, one of the newly created territories in this purchase, an area now known as the state of Missouri, asked to be admitted to the Union as a slave state. This request caused an uproar. At the time, there was a balance of power in the U.S. Senate, the number of senators from eleven free states and eleven slave states being equal. If Missouri was admitted as a slave state, the Southern states would have two more senators than the North did, and this was not acceptable to Northern congressmen.

Eventually, the crisis was resolved by bringing in Maine, which had been part of Massachusetts, as a free state, thereby keeping the balance. To end the debate over the spread of slavery, Congress divided the rest of the purchase along the 36°30′ parallel. Territories entering the Union north of this line would be free; those south of the line could have slaves if they chose to do so. This agreement was known as the Compromise of 1820; it is often referred to today as the "Missouri Compromise."

Even though lawmakers had thought that they had settled the spread-of-slavery issue once and for all, they were sadly mistaken. In 1846, the United States declared war on Mexico. When this conflict ended two years later, the United States reaffirmed its claim to Texas, which had successfully fought for independence from Mexico in 1836 and had been added to the United States in 1845 despite vigorous objections from the Mexican government. The United States also took control of what is now California, New Mexico, Arizona, Nevada, and Utah, as well as parts of Wyoming and Colorado.

Now another act regarding the spread of slavery was needed. After long and heated debates during which the breakup of the Union was again threatened, Congress finally passed the Compromise of 1850. This agreement allowed any territories carved out of the land taken from Mexico (other than California, which would enter the Union as a free state to offset Texas's entry as a slave state) to decide if they would permit slavery within their borders. This compromise also called for stricter enforcement of a fugitive slave law to help Southerners reclaim their property. Since it was unlikely that the United States would be adding any territory in the near future, Congress hoped—once again—that its debate over slavery had ended.

But as Southerners looked about them, they saw little opportunity to continue to add slave states, which was crucial if they wanted to maintain a balance of power in Congress. Extending slavery further west into the newly acquired lands was not practical. No one could raise cotton or tobacco in the desert, for example, at least not without extensive and expensive irrigation systems. So Southerners looked longingly at Cuba, Nicaragua, and even parts of Mexico and dreamed about acquiring territories there and making them into slave states. Meanwhile, Southerners decided to fight for every inch of land—even land that had been declared off limits—that might realistically be made into slave territory. This included Kansas.

In 1854, some Northern businessmen envisioned a railroad route from Chicago to the West Coast, and they asked Congress to officially establish the Kansas and Nebraska territories through which the route would run. Northern congressmen were eager for a new railroad, since it would make travel and transporting goods between the coasts for their voters so much easier. Therefore many of them eagerly supported Senator Stephen A. Douglas when he introduced a bill to organize the territories. To get Southern representatives whose states would benefit little from a Northern railroad to vote for Douglas's Kansas-Nebraska bill, Northern leaders in Congress agreed to give the settlers in the territories, both of which had been declared free in 1820 because they were north of the 36°30′ line, the right to have slaves if the voters in the territories decided to do so. This was known as popular sovereignty.

Stephen A. Douglas

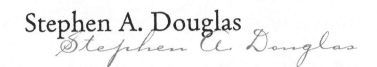

Stephen Arnold Douglas. Courtesy of the Library of Congress

Stephen A. Douglas introduced his Kansas-Nebraska bill, one of the most controversial pieces of legislation in American history, to the Senate in 1854. Douglas, who had had a long political career in state politics in Illinois before he was elected to the U.S. House of Representatives in 1843, believed in national expansion. He had fought for the annexation of Texas and had supported the war with Mexico. His interest in expansion had led to a special appointment in the House: chairman of the Committee on Territories. When he was elected to the Senate in 1847, he chaired the Senate's Committee on Territories. As a result, Douglas was a powerful man, and even though he barely reached five feet in height, he was called the "Little Giant."

Historians have long argued about Douglas's motives in reopening the slavery issue in the Kansas and Nebraska territories. Some believe that he was seeking personal monetary gain, since he owned land that potentially could have been part of the railroad project. Others think that he was simply trying to prevent a bitter debate over slavery in Congress. The majority, though, suspect that he already had his eye on the presidency, and needing the support of Southern Democrats to win, he had drafted legislation that would please the South. Whatever his reason—or reasons—might have been, Douglas was very persuasive, and his bill became law on May 22, 1854.

But his victory cost him dearly. Angry citizens held what they called "indignation meetings" all over the North, during which they burned effigies of the senator. So many were set ablaze night after night that Douglas noted that he could have found his way from Washington, D.C., to Illinois just by the light of the flames.

Believing, correctly, that they were losing ground, angry abolitionists and Northerners who opposed the spread of slavery into new
territories, free soilers, joined forces. They thought enough was enough! They would make a test case of Kansas. Just as determined,
Southerners sought volunteers who would settle in the territory and
vote for slavery. Southern leaders now believed that if they lost Kansas,
they might never gain another state for their side, which would eventually give the North more and more power in the legislature, putting
slavery, one of the South's most valued institutions, at great risk.

Senator David Atchison of Missouri, serving as U.S. senator from
that state since 1843, led the proslavery forces. He had at least two reasons for wanting Kansas to become a slave state. First, he was afraid that
if Kansas become a free state, slaves all along the western border in
Missouri would try to escape to Kansas, where they would receive food,
shelter, and advice on how best to remain free. Second, Atchison, like
many Missourians who thought of Kansas as their own backyard,
regarded the abolitionists and free soilers as intruders. If they wanted
to settle a new territory, he shouted, let them move to Nebraska!

Atchison had been elected president *pro tempore* of the U.S. Senate sixteen times. He had also served as vice president of the United
States from April 18, 1853, to December 4, 1854, after President
Franklin Pierce's vice president, William King, died in office. In short,
Atchison was a powerful leader, and when he issued the first call,
Southerners paid him heed. "Citizens of the West, South, and Illinois!"
he exclaimed. "Stake out your claims and woe be to the Abolitionist . . .
who shall intrude upon it or come within reach of your long and true
rifles, or within point blank shot of your revolvers."[5]

Senator William Seward of New York took up the challenge.
"Come on then, gentlemen of the slave states! Since there is no escap-
ing your challenge, I accept it, in behalf of freedom. We will engage in
competition for the virgin soil of Kansas and God give victory to the
side that is stronger in numbers as it is in right."[6]

Chapter Three

SETTLERS ON A MISSION

The first "settlers" to arrive in Kansas were from Missouri. Few really meant to stay; they simply wanted to claim the land for the proslavery cause. So on June 10, 1854, they marched into the Salt Creek valley in Kansas, announced that from then on Kansas was slave territory, and staked out some sites. Some of the men began modest foundations for cabins to make the claims appear valid, and then after a few rocks were in place, they posted signs to keep antislavery people away. These messages were anything but subtle. Threats—"If I find any damned rascal tearing this foundation down, I'll cut his liver out"[7]—were very common.

Many of the first Missourians in Kansas were frontiersmen who had strong ties to the territory. They had hunted on its plains, explored its river bottoms, and camped in its hills. Frontiersmen also took great pride in their rough-and-tumble ways, insisting that they could swear louder, shoot better, and drink more than any other men east of the Rocky Mountains. These men, eventually known as "border ruffians," a term they relished, hooted at the very thought of pantywaist Yankees trying to settle in

Kansas. There wasn't a Yankee in the entire East, ruffians declared, who was tough enough to endure a Kansas summer or winter.

Although much had been written about Kansas by westward-bound emigrants on their way to California or Oregon, most of what had been recorded in letters and journals was about the beauty of the land, not the climate. Emigrants, who usually passed through the area in late spring or very early summer, recorded seeing mile upon mile of lush green grass and masses of wildflowers in every color imaginable. But smug frontiersmen knew that summer temperatures in the area could reach 90°F, even 100°F, by mid-summer, then remain hot and humid for months. Not only was the heat uncomfortable, it was dangerous, for it promoted diseases such as cholera that could fell even the toughest ruffian. Emigrants also didn't realize that the winters could be incredibly cold; temperatures could plummet to -30°F when gale-force winds swept down from the north, making staying alive a real challenge.

Wanting to make certain that the proslavery cause was off to a really good start, and not willing to put all their faith in the severe climate to stop the Yankees, the frontiersmen, then more and more Missourians, established three towns: Leavenworth, Kickapoo, and Atchison. Atchison was named for Senator David Atchison, who had issued the call to every Southerner to head to Kansas and make it a slave state.

The Missourians were joined shortly after by Southerners from South Carolina, Georgia, Alabama, and Mississippi, many of whom did not own slaves. Although these settlers were Southern sympathizers to the core, they, like a number of Northerners rushing into the territory, simply wanted a piece of inexpensive land, where they could make a fresh start in peace and quiet.

Meanwhile Yankees were making preparations to move to Kansas. Although some made the trek on their own, most traveled with an emigrant company. These companies were financed by wealthy industrialists in the East, who vowed to send at least twenty thousand settlers to

Kansas in 1854

Kansas in 1854

W hen the first settlers arrived in the newly opened Kansas Territory, they were not entering a strange and unknown area. This territory had been thoroughly explored, first in the early 1500s by Spanish conquistadors such as Francisco Vasquez de Coronado, and later, after the Louisiana Purchase had been made, by Captains Meriwether Lewis, William Clark, and Zebulon M. Pike.

In addition, two major trails crossed the territory, both of which were heavily traveled at the time. One of these routes, the Santa Fe Trail, was used primarily by traders who brought goods from the Southwest to markets in the North. The second, the Oregon Trail, was used by emigrants going west to Oregon and California.

Also, the area was well known to various Indian tribes. Besides the Kansa, Osage, Wichita, and Pawnee Indians, who had long lived in Kansas, in 1830 the territory had become home to more than eleven thousand Indians from the East who had been forcibly removed from their homelands. These Indians included members of the Kickapoo, Shawnee, Delaware, Pottawatomie, Wyandotte, Ottawa, Chippewa, Iowa, Miami, Sac, and Fox nations. Priests and ministers had followed the Indians to Kansas, where they had started a number of missions, several of which, such as the Shawnee Mission, flourished. As the result of a series of treaties, many of the

Indians in Kansas were moved further west just before the area became a territory, as Congress laid the groundwork for white settlement.

To protect the trails and the people using them from Indian attacks, the U.S. government built three forts in Kansas, Fort Leavenworth (1827), Fort Scott (1842), and Fort Riley (1852). Small settlements sprang up around the forts, but in 1854 they were little more than primitive outposts.

Kansas each year. Each company raised money by charging members a fee to join, usually $1, and selling stock in the company. The society or company used the money it raised to send workers in advance of the settlers to start towns. The advance workers built boardinghouses, where settlers would live until their homes could be completed, and sawmills and gristmills to provide lumber and feed. Eventually, the companies hoped to sell their property, mills, for example, at a profit, which would then be shared by all stockholders.

Many different companies sprang up almost overnight. One of the most unusual was the Vegetarian Settlement Company. Not only did members have to sign a statement swearing that they were not slaveholders, they had to agree not to smoke, drink liquor, or eat meat in any form. This company was slow to provide for its settlers, and many had to spend their first summer in the territory living in tents.

The site the Vegetarian Settlement Company chose had incredibly rich soil, though, and the settlers eventually raised bumper crops. Miriam Colt, one of the company's members, noted in her journal on June 17, 1855, her second summer in Kansas Territory, that the crops were doing especially well. She wrote, "The soil of rich layers of vegetable mould is throwing up the rows of dark green blades of corn. [Our] cornfield of six acres looks promising, as do all the cornfields around. Pumpkins, squashes, melons, cucumbers, beans, peas, potatoes, and tomatoes are thriving finely."[8]

The first free-soil town to be established was Lawrence, which was named after Amos Lawrence, a wealthy merchant and philanthropist and a leader in the New England Emigrant Aid Society, the largest and best-known of the societies. This settlement was started by twenty-nine Yankees who were a real contrast to the border ruffians. These settlers, all male, were highly educated—doctors, teachers, ministers, and such—who toted Bibles under their arms.

The Emigrant Aid Society, looking for volunteers to go to Kansas, did everything it could to publicize its cause. It was so successful at this that the first settlers, regarded as heroes who would stand up against the evils of slavery, were sent off with great fanfare. According to Eli Thayer, one of the leaders of the company:

> This pioneer colony left Boston on the 17th of July, 1854. Immense crowds had gathered at the station to give them the parting godspeed and the pledge of their future cordial care. They moved out of the station amid the cheering crowds who lined the track for several blocks. The fact of this intense public interest impelled others to prepare to join the colony, intending to go one month later. . . . The emigrants remained in Worcester [Massachusetts] the first night and received a suitable ovation. . . . The next day I took charge of the party, and we were met in the evening at Albany [New York] by a good number of the citizens, who welcomed us with great cordiality. The next day we were cheered at all the principal stations as we passed on our westward journey.[9]

This company sent a second group of settlers, sixty-seven men, women and children, to Lawrence in August. A third group departed in late September.

But even though the society tried its best to provide for the settlers, it could not keep up with the demand for housing. As a result, some settlers were forced to live in partially finished homes that were little more than four walls, a roof, and a dirt floor. To keep out the insects in summer and the cold in winter, these settlers covered their windows and doorways with old calico, heavy blankets, or buffalo robes, which they bought from local Indians for $4 apiece, approximately half a week's average salary then, or exchanged for a hefty supply of sugar and flour.

Until the settlers' belongings, which the companies helped transport, arrived, furnishings in the cabins were simple. Emigrants sewed sheets together and stuffed the cases with dried grass to serve as mattresses. Settlers also used clothing trunks for chairs and tables, and put their names on waiting lists for the greatest of all luxuries, an iron stove.

Because they ran short of supplies, many of the first settlers were not prepared for the hard winter that followed, just as the border ruffians had predicted. One settler recalled:

> Yesterday we were greeted by a pretty severe snow-storm, for which we were hardly prepared. . . . This morning I crawled from under my buffalo skin, after having . . . [a] pile of snow . . . for a bed. I kindled a fire in our rough stone fire place, but the smoke rolled in upon us at such a rate, that we were compelled to remove the fire, not to the middle of the floor, but where the middle of the floor would be if we only had a floor. By doing this we could get to the windward of the fire and thus avoid the smoke. If you could only see a true picture of us now, as we are seated upon a trunk beside the fire, with our feet extended to keep them warm, and a large tool chest at our backs, with the lid raised to break the wind and a buffalo pelt drawn closely about us.[10]

Once Lawrence was thought to be secure, emigrant companies sent volunteers to other locations. Eventually these sites became modern day Topeka, Manhattan, and Osawatomie.

Besides providing the bare necessities for settlers when they arrived, emigrant societies also provided inexpensive transportation and guides for the groups. This made the journey to Kansas much safer, especially for the wives and children who followed, but it did not guarantee an easy trip.

Hannah Ropes journeyed to Kansas a year after Lawrence was established with a group of twenty-five people, including ten children and five other women. Her son Edward had already settled in Kansas, where he had started a cabin for himself, his mother, and his sister, who traveled westward with Hannah. Although Ropes was not one of the first emigrants to go to Kansas, her travel experiences were typical, and

Hannah Anderson Ropes moved to Kansas in 1855. She was deeply opposed to the spread of slavery and used her political connections—she knew several U.S. senators—to help further the free soil cause in the territory. The photo was taken in 1862. Courtesy of the University of California, Riverside

unlike many travelers, she left a detailed account of her trip, *Six Months in Kansas.*

As did most emigrants from New England, she and the others in her group boarded a train in Boston. After numerous transfers from one train to another, they reached the end of the line, several hundred miles short of the Kansas border. There settlers boarded a steamboat, which carried them westward and across Missouri on the Missouri River. Emigrants made the rest of the trip in carriages or wagons.

Hannah's group left Boston on September 11, 1855, and arrived in Lawrence on September 20. During her journey, Ropes recorded her experiences in a lengthy letter to her mother. Hannah added something to her missive almost every day.

> *September 12th*—The hope of a good night's rest at Albany [New York] kept us up till eleven o'clock. We were stiff and tired, and the children cross. . . . We [were taken to] a dimly-lighted parlor. . . . Chairs were brought, enough for all; the gas [lamp] was turned up more brilliantly; a pitcher of water and one [glass] were procured; the hands of the timepiece pointed to twelve. O, how tired we were! Would the clerk never show us our beds? He came in very pleasantly, and remarked, with as much composure as though he was speaking of the weather; "Every bed in the house is full. You must make yourselves comfortable till breakfast time!"
>
> *[September 13]* Now we whirl along opposite Detroit. . . . All sorts of unearthly sounds are about us; and people of every nation seem to be hurrying west.
>
> *[September 14]* At five o'clock we took seats for Illinois; rode all night at a furious rate; got out at Lake Station before daylight, and were huddled into a dirty room to wait till seven. I have seen nothing clean to eat, drink, or sit or stand upon for some time.
>
> *[September 18]* It is just a week since we left home, and we are [on a steamer] three hundred and fifty miles up [the Missouri River]. . . . Tomorrow we have the promise of being in Kansas City [Missouri].
>
> *[September 19]* We passed the night comfortably; and as early as teams could be procured, started towards Kansas Territory. Our carriage was a cart, covered with sail-cloth, not quite high enough to allow us to sit with our heads up.
>
> *[September 20]* Soon [our driver] tells us to . . . look at the city at our feet. One could hardly conceive of a picture so really *beautiful*,

of a town one year old. As we enter, the river—which we do not see—forms the background, with its thickly-wooded bank. A few nice-looking houses appear, and cabins quite numberless. We ride to the door of the Cincinnati House [a boardinghouse]. And now, my dear mother, my journey is over. I tie my [bonnet] and with a nervous, trembling hand, say good-bye.[11]

Hannah joined a growing number of antislavery emigrants in the territory. When she arrived there would have been almost ten thousand settlers. About two-thirds of these citizens were women and children.

Border ruffians watched these antislavery settlements with growing alarm. Hoping to drive the settlers away, ruffians shook their fists, hurled threats, and insisted that the Northerners leave. The Northerners, to the ruffians' great surprise, not only refused to pull up stakes and head back East, they began toting rifles under their arms along with their Bibles. The two sides then eyed each other uneasily, digging in their heels, clearly determined to claim Kansas for their side. What wasn't as clear was who the winner would be.

Chapter Four

VOTERS ON THE MOVE

Shortly after Kansas Territory was established, President Franklin Pierce asked Andrew H. Reeder from Pennsylvania to be its governor. Reeder, who was a staunch believer in popular sovereignty, traveled to Kansas at a very leisurely pace, arriving at Fort Leavenworth in October, nearly four months after he had received the appointment. After exploring part of the territory to acquaint himself with the lay of the land, Reeder announced his plans for establishing a government in Kansas. These plans included electing a territorial delegate to Congress on November 29, 1854, and selecting a territorial legislature the following spring.

Meanwhile, a judicial system was being put in place. President Pierce appointed Samuel Lecompte, a slaveholder, as chief justice of the territory's supreme court. He was to be assisted by two judges, Rush Elmore, another slaveholder, and Sanders Johnson, who supported popular sovereignty.

Proslavery supporters were not happy about waiting until spring to elect representatives to the legislature. These settlers wanted to have the elections as soon as possible, while they still commanded a majority in the territory. They had already seen too many abolitionists as well as numerous free soilers who stood firm against the spread of slavery flowing into Kansas, and the aid societies' threat of sending at least twenty thousand settlers per year worried them.

But proslavery forces had little to fret about. Senator Atchison had already made plans to help them beat back the brazen intruders. Long before Governor Reeder had arrived, Atchison had begun to organize secret aid societies in Missouri as well as in other parts of the South to promote slavery in Kansas and any other new territory to be opened in the future. These societies, known as Sons of the South and Blue Lodges, claimed more than five thousand members in Missouri, all of whom swore to promote slavery.

In November, Atchison began to put one of his boldest plots into action: Missourians would vote in the election in Kansas to make sure that the right—that is, a proslavery—representative was chosen. Atchison spoke before many crowds along the Missouri-Kansas border to drum up support. "Now if a set of fanatics and demagogues a thousand miles off," he began, "can afford to advance the money and extend every nerve to abolitionize the territory and exclude the slaveholder . . . what is your duty? When you reside one day's journey to the territory . . . you can, without exertion, send five hundred of your young men who will vote in favor of your institutions."[12]

Enthusiastic and heavily armed Missourians poured across the border on voting day to cast their ballots, and these men elected General J.W. Whitfield, who lived in Missouri at the time, as the territory's delegate to Congress. Needless to say, antislavery settlers were furious. When Governor Reeder announced that he would not recognize Whitfield as the winner nor would the governor tolerate such action in the future, slaveholders' eyebrows shot up all over the country. They had expected an appointee of President Pierce's to be more supportive of slavery.

Even though they had lost the first election, most Northerners in Kansas eventually calmed themselves, then looked ahead. By the time the next election rolled around, federal officials, as they had in other territories, would be in place to supervise the balloting. Those

David Rice Atchison, a senator from Missouri and a former acting vice president of the United States, was one of the leaders of the border ruffians. Courtesy of the Library of Congress

David Rice Atchison

Missourians, abolitionists and free soilers muttered, may have won the first round, but they would certainly lose the next one.

Shortly after, as expected, federal officials arrived to help prepare for the spring balloting. They began by dividing the territory into districts, each of which included proslavery supporters, abolitionists, and free soilers, who together were to elect a representative to the territorial legislature. Then officials took a headcount. They recorded 8,501 settlers (men, women, and children). Of these, 5,128 were males and 3,373 were females, who could not vote. The officials also noted that there were 242 slaves in the territory. Of the more than five thousand males, only 2,905 were old enough to cast a ballot.

Although the abolitionists were certain that the next election would be fair, they were wrong. Since illegal voters had worked so well before, Missourians said, why not repeat the process? Senator Atchison, not content to just round up a few ruffians, ran up and down western Missouri, enlisting even more border-crossing voters than before.

Atchison was backed by Dr. John Stringfellow, a former Missourian and editor of the Atchison proslavery newspaper, the *Squatter Sovereign,* who had returned to Missouri to help the senator. Stringfellow believed that the very practice of slavery was at stake. Let the abolitionists and free soilers win Kansas, he reasoned, and they would be so emboldened that they would not stop at limiting the spread of slavery; instead, they would try to free every slave in the South. Because he believed so much was at stake, he advocated violence if necessary, which did not offend some of the ruffians. "I advise you one and all to enter every election district in Kansas, in defiance of Reeder and his vile [followers], and vote at the point of Bowie knife or revolver!"[13]

To make voting easier for Missourians, Stringfellow, Atchison, and their supporters promised every man who would cross the border and vote on March 30 a free ferry ride across the Missouri River, a dollar a day for expenses, and abundant liquor. These expenses were funded by the Blue Lodges, a number of which collected money from slaveholders scattered throughout the South.

The flood of voters from Missouri began two days before the election. In fact, so many Missourians showed up that the ferries couldn't handle all of them. To make sure that every man who wanted to vote got an opportunity to do so, Atchison had an extra vessel pressed into service. And to make sure that the Kansans understood that these men meant business, the would-be voters toted guns and dragged two cannons behind them.

The Missourians were not only determined, they were well organized. Leaders of the lodges divided the volunteers into groups and sent them in overwhelming numbers to specific sites to cast ballots, wherever proslavery people believed that the election results might be in doubt. For example, more than one thousand Missourians were sent to Lawrence, which at the time had less than five hundred citizens. Here

Missourians flocked to Kansas in 1855 to vote in the territorial elections. Courtesy of the Kansas State Historical Society, Topeka, Kansas

the Missourians rode into town in parade-like fashion, banging on drums to announce their arrival and holding banners high in the air.

On election day, the Missourians marched into the polling sites and demanded to be given ballots. Any judge or official who balked was told to resign and let one of the Missourians handle the voting. If he wouldn't do so, the Missourians said, patting their sidearms, he would die. By the end of the day, only 1,414 registered voters had cast their ballots, yet there was a total of 6,307 ballots in the boxes, the vast majority of which supported proslavery candidates.

Proslavery supporters hailed the victory. The editor of the *Leavenworth Herald*, a proslavery paper, wrote, "ALL HAIL! Proslavery Party Victorious! Come on, Southern men! Bring your slaves and fill up the Territory. Kansas is saved. Abolitionism is rebuked, her fortress stormed, her flag is dragging in the dust!"[14]

Governor Reeder was appalled. He had promised a fair election, and he had not been able to deliver it. So to undo the damage, Reeder declared the election null and void and scheduled yet another vote on May 22.

Reeder's decision enraged proslavery forces. They tried to stop the election by threatening Reeder's life. When threats failed to accomplish their goal, some ruffians made examples out of the men who had complained of fraud. One of the victims was William Phillips, a lawyer in Lawrence. Ruffians seized Phillips, then took him to Missouri, where they tarred and feathered him and sold him as a slave in a mock auction. After enduring these dangerous humiliations and repeated threats on his life, Phillips was set free.

In the election on May 22, fewer Missourians crossed the border to vote. As a result, eleven free soilers (out of a total of 39 elected representatives) actually won seats in the new legislature. This was not a problem for proslavery forces, however; they had made plans for this possibility more than a month before. When the legislature convened in July in Pawnee, heavily armed proslavery legislators simply refused to accept the free soilers, arguing that the first, not the second, election was legitimate. Now Governor Reeder was even more upset, but there was little he could do.

The legislature quickly passed a series of laws that protected slavery. From then on, it was illegal to even question the practice of slavery in Kansas. Anyone caught helping a slave escape was to receive the death penalty, and the governor was stripped of his ability to issue pardons in such cases, thereby making sure that the penalty would stick. Reeder vetoed the bills, but the proslavery legislature overrode his vetoes.

The first legislative session was brief. Pawnee had no facilities for the legislators, so the men had to live in tents and cook their own food over open fires. The July heat was excessive, and there were no trees to provide shade for lunch or afternoon breaks, greatly increasing the men's discomfort. So when rumors of a cholera outbreak nearby began to circulate, legislators were only too glad to use the threat as an excuse to move to another site. On July 16, the men reconvened at the Shawnee Mission.

The struggle between Governor Reeder and the territory's legislature did not go unnoticed, nor did it please supporters of slavery elsewhere. As a result, many proslavery leaders in the Democratic Party put pressure on President Pierce, who like most politicians hoped to run for re-election, arguing that Reeder couldn't govern the territory effectively. What they meant was that Reeder was fighting proslavery efforts and this was unacceptable. When speculation about some of Reeder's land dealings cast doubt on his honesty, Pierce used the incident as a reason to fire the governor on July 28, 1855.

Proslavery supporters celebrated Pierce's decision. They were certain now that the slavery issue in Kansas was under control and in their favor. They shouldn't have been so confident: The struggle was far from over.

Chapter Five

THAT'S TREASON!

Frustrated and angry at their lack of progress, free soilers and abolitionists vented their feelings at numerous meetings held in late July and August of 1855. Not only was their cherished goal of making Kansas a free state currently at risk, they could see no way in which they could hope to change things through the political system. No one represented them in the territorial legislature, and the new governor, Wilson Shannon from Ohio, not only accepted the first election results, he refused to meet with free soilers, even on a social basis. Worse yet, the laws passed by the proslavery legislature took away Kansans' right to speak out against slavery. This was supposed to eliminate the possibility of any antislavery candidate campaigning for office. And most frightening of all, free soilers and abolitionists were barred from serving on juries, making a fair trial, should one of them be arrested, highly questionable.

Some speakers at these meetings, unwilling to be cowed by the proslavery legislature, wanted much more than an opportunity to air their complaints. They hoped to provoke and embolden their listeners. These speakers insisted that their listeners' basic rights as Americans had been violated. What happened to freedom of speech? they shouted. And what about the right to be represented? They repeatedly recalled how their ancestors had fought the British to gain their rights. Wasn't this, they asked, a similar situation? And didn't events in the territory, as they had in the colonies back in 1776, demand bold action?

Eventually those who wanted to be rid of the proslavery government joined forces to form the Free State party, which was a risky venture. Members included men from the various aid companies, even the vegetarians; radical abolitionists, such as John Brown, who had just arrived in the territory; free soilers; and one of the most colorful characters in the area, James Lane.

Lane, a tall, thin man with a shock of dark hair that refused to stay in place, commanded attention the moment he entered a room. Besides being physically striking, he was a dramatic speaker, and his presentations, full of gestures and exaggerated facial expressions, could actually bring audiences to their feet, even when he didn't believe a word of what he was saying.

His ability to persuade others had served him well in the past. Lane had successfully led two volunteer regiments during the war with Mexico (1846 - 1848), and after returning to his home state of Indiana, he had used his military experience and his ability to lead to launch a political career. He had served as his state's lieutenant governor from 1849 to 1853 and as a Democratic member of the U.S. House of Representatives from Indiana from 1853 to1855. While in Congress, Lane had supported the Kansas-Nebraska bill, which had enraged his constituents, the majority of whom wanted to limit the spread of slavery. No amount of persuasion, even when Lane was at his best, could convince the good citizens of Indiana to send him back to Congress, and as a result, in 1855 his plan to become a senator was in shambles.

Believing that events in Kansas might give his floundering career a boost, Lane headed west, where he offered his support to the proslavery cause. But most proslavery leaders, to Lane's mortification, were hesitant to accept his help. Not only did they question his sincerity—after all, he was a Northerner—they also saw a mighty competitor in

Lane, whose political ambitions threatened them. Miffed but unwilling to give up on his plan, Lane then did a complete about-face: He joined the opposition.

Needless to say, Free Staters were just as skeptical about Lane's sincerity as proslavery forces had been, so he had to persuade them that he had indeed seen the error of his ways when he had tried to join the Southern camp. At numerous meetings during the summer of 1855, Lane took the stage, delivering some of his best speeches. He would shout at the top of his lungs one moment, drop his voice to a whisper the next, and ridicule his opponents with well-chosen words that delighted his audiences.

A reporter for the *Kansas City Times* (Missouri) followed Lane, recording his impression of this most unusual man. After one of Lane's most rousing speeches, the reporter said:

> The crowd was immense. The hour came and the people to hear. Lane was in his best mood. He was prepared for a vituperative, sarcastic, ironical and intensely personal speech. . . . His late . . . associates were denounced, burlesqued, ridiculed and pilloried in a hysteria of laughter by an excited, cyclonic crowd. No one ever afterward doubted where Lane stood.[15]

The first official meeting of the Free State party, one hundred delegates in all, including Lane, took place on September 5, 1855, in Big Springs, a small village west of Lawrence. While these representatives debated and discussed, they were observed by more than three hundred interested spectators, who had come to watch history being made.

The delegates made a number of decisions that amounted to nothing less than a declaration of independence from those in power in Kansas. While spectators held their breath, one delegate after another declared that the current legislature was not representative of Kansans, and therefore not worthy of support. It was nothing more than a bogus government elected by people who weren't citizens. Free

This photo of James Lane and his wife was probably taken shortly after he became a U.S. senator in 1861. Note Mrs. Lane's full skirt and bonnet and James Lane's cloak, typical clothing in the mid-1800s. Courtesy of the National Archives

James Lane and his wife

Staters, delegates insisted, should form a government of their own. Representatives then agreed to hold a constitutional convention on October 23 in Topeka, which was to be the official capital of the Free State party, to lay the groundwork.

In addition, the convention, wanting and needing a representative in Washington, nominated former governor Andrew Reeder for office. Reeder had thrown himself into the Free State movement with great vigor and determination after President Pierce had fired him. Until delegates could meet again, members of the convention recommended that Free Staters begin to form militias for their defense, just as the colonists had done in the 1770s.

Long before the Free Staters met in Big Springs, the proslavery legislature had designated October 1 as the day to elect a territorial representative. J. W. Whitfield, who had won the first election held almost one year before, was chosen to be the proslavery party's candidate again. On October 1, Whitfield, with the help of some Missourians, received more than three thousand votes.

Eight days later, Free Staters, who wanted nothing to do with the October 1 election, went to their polls. Because there were more antislavery settlers in the territory than before, Andrew Reeder received more votes in this election than Whitfield had in his. As a result, Free Staters declared Reeder the real winner. Neither side would acknowledge the other's election results, so both men went to Washington, introducing themselves as the rightful delegate from Kansas. The U.S. House of Representatives refused to seat either candidate, claiming that both elections were irregular at best.

On October 23, Free State delegates met in Topeka as planned. Under the leadership of James Lane, the representatives drafted a constitution that established a legislature and a court system. Delegates also discussed electing their own governor.

One of the men mentioned for nomination was Dr. Charles Robinson. Robinson had served as a physician and a teacher in his native state of Massachusetts before heading to California during the 1849 gold rush. He had been a leader in one of the squatters' association near

THE DAY OF
OUR ENSLAVEMENT!!

To-day, Sept. 15, 1855, is the day on which the iniquitous enactment of an illegitimate, illegal and fraudulent Legislature have declared commences the prostration of the Right of Speech and the curtailment of the LIBERTY OF THE PRESS!! To-day commences an Era in Kansas which, unless the sturdy voice of the People, backed, if necessary, by "strong arms and the sure eye," shall teach the tyrants who attempt to enthrall us the lesson which our Fathers taught to kingly tyrants of old, shall prostrate us in the dust, and make us the slaves of an Oligarchy

Worse than the veriest Despotism on Earth!

To-day commences the operation of a law which declares: "Sec. 12. If any free person, by speaking or by writing, assert or maintain that persons have not the right to hold slaves in this Territory, or shall introduce into this Territory, print, publish, write, circulate or cause to be introduced into this Territory, written, printed, published or circulated in this Territory, any book, paper, magazine, pamphlet or circular, containing any denial of the right of persons to hold slaves in this Territory, such person shall be deemed guilty of Felony, and punished by imprisonment at hard labor for a term of not less than two years."

Now we DO ASSERT and we declare, despite all the bolts and bars of the iniquitous Legislature of Kansas, that

"PERSONS HAVE NOT THE
RIGHT TO HOLD SLAVES IN THIS TERRITORY."

And we will emblazon it upon our banner in letters so large and in language so plain that the infatuated invaders who elected the Kansas Legislature, as well as

THAT CORRUPT AND IGNORANT LEGISLATURE

Itself, may understand it—so that, if they cannot read, they may SPELL IT OUT, and meditate and deliberate upon it; and we hold that the man who fails to utter this self-evident truth, on account of the insolent enactment alluded to, is a poltroon and a slave worse than the black slaves of our persecutors and oppressors.

The Constitution of the United States, the great Magna Charta of American Liberties,

Guarantees to every Citizen the Liberty of Speech and the Freedom of the Press!

And this is the first time in the history of America that a body claiming Legislative powers has dared to attempt to wrest them from the people. And it is not only the right, but the bounden duty of every Freeman to spurn with contempt and trample under foot an enactment which thus basely violates the rights of Freemen. For our part we DO and SHALL CONTINUE to utter this truth so long as we have the power of utterance, and nothing but the brute force of an overbearing tyranny can prevent us.

Will any citizen — any free American — brook the insult of

AN INSOLENT GAG LAW!!

the work of a Legislature elected by bullying ruffians who invaded Kansas with arms, and whose drunken revelry, and insults to our peaceable, law-abiding, and comparatively unarmed citizens, were a disgrace to manhood, and a burlesque upon popular Republican Government! If they do, they are slaves already, and with them Freedom is but a mockery.

Courtesy of Kansas State Historical Society, Topeka, Kansas

The Day of Our Enslavement

Sacramento, and when fights had broken out over land claims, he had been seriously wounded. Many considered his work in the association to be nothing less than heroic, and as a result, he had been elected to California's house of representatives, where he served one term (1850-1851) before returning to Massachusetts. In 1854, Robinson had become swept up in the struggle to make Kansas a free state. He had joined the Massachusetts Emigrant Aid Society, and after leading a group of settlers to Kansas, he had become the society's chief agent in the territory.

Now, in 1855, Dr. Robinson was one of the driving forces behind the Free State party. Throughout the summer, he spoke to as many groups as possible, trying to unite the many factions within the territory. As he spoke, he often compared the free soilers' and abolitionists' struggle to the colonists' struggle in 1776. One of the best examples of such a speech was given at a Fourth of July celebration. Robinson said, in part:

> Fellow-citizens . . . it is for us to choose for ourselves, and for those who shall come after us, what institutions shall bless or curse our beautiful Kansas. Shall we have freedom for all the people . . . or slavery for a part? Choose ye this day which you will serve— slavery or Freedom—and then be true to your choice.
>
> Let every man stand in his place, and acquit himself like a man who knows his rights, and knowing, dares maintain them. Let us repudiate all laws enacted by [bogus] legislative bodies. . . . Tyrants are tyrants, and tyranny is tyranny. . . . So thought and so acted our ancestors; and so let us think and act. We are not alone in this contest. The entire nation is agitated upon the question of our rights; the spirit of '76 is breathing upon some. . . . I seem to hear the millions of freemen, and the millions of bondsmen [slaves] . . . the patriots . . . the spirits of the revolutionary heroes, and the voice of God, all saying to the people of Kansas, "Do your duty!"[16]

In addition to laying the groundwork for a government, representatives in Topeka included a controversial plank in their constitution, at Lane's insistence, that forbade any blacks, slave or free, from living in Kansas. The anti-black law was a concession to settlers who feared that free blacks would work for low wages, potentially hurting poor whites in the territory. Also, Free Staters believed that this move might mollify proslavery forces, proving once and for all that Northern settlers—at least most of them—were not out to harbor fugitive slaves.

Delegates decided to submit the constitution to the people of the territory on December 15. If accepted, it would make Kansas Territory unique in American history. Not only would it be the only

Sara Robinson

Sara Robinson (signature)

Sara Robinson. Courtesy of the Kansas State Historical
Society, Topeka, Kansas

Sara Tappan Doolittle Lawrence Robinson, the wife of Dr.
Charles Robinson, was one of the best-known and most vocal
women in Kansas Territory. While her husband struggled to
outwit proslavery forces, Sara entertained guests, nursed her
sick neighbors, and took careful notes about the political
events in Kansas, which she eventually published in 1856 in a

book titled *Kansas: Its Interior and Exterior Life.* This book is full of descriptions of visitors to her home, her neighbors, the weather, the status of various crops, who was ill and dying, and celebrations the women in Lawrence planned. This gives us a better understanding of what life was like in Kansas Territory, proof that it wasn't all political intrigue.

July 4th [1855]—The morning of the Fourth came in cloudy, yet pleasant. Word had been sent to the people [along] the Wakarusa [River] and many were expected. Invitations also were sent to the Delaware and Shawnee Indians to mingle in our festivities. From the elevated position of our house we saw the people gathering from all quarters. Several teams of oxen as well as horses, the roughness of the vehicles being hidden under garlands of green leaves and flowers, came in from the Wakarusa. A beautiful flag was presented by a Massachusetts lady to the military companies of Lawrence. . . . After its acceptance, the procession formed upon Massachusetts Street and was escorted by the military to a fine grove about a mile from town. Here, in one of Nature's grand old forests, seats had been provided, and a platform raised for the orators and other speakers, for the singers and musical instruments. The number present was variously estimated from fifteen hundred to two thousand.

Nov. 15th [1855]—Rainy and very chilly. . . . For two or three days men have been out in the woods hunting game; and to-night a large number of our citizens have gathered to partake of the supper, and join in the general festivities of the hour. Notwithstanding the rain, the mud being over [our] shoes in depth, at an early hour the large dining-hall of the hotel was full of people, our neighbors and friends, while many came from miles away. A piano stood at the upper end of the room—parlor and dining-hall being thrown into one—and over the arch of the folding doors waved the [flag presented on July 4]. The tables occupying the length of the hall, in double rows, were loaded with wild game, rabbits, squirrels, prairie-chickens, turkeys and one porker . . . while cakes of every variety, with pastry, grace the table. All this cooking was done by one lady—one of the earliest settlers. . . . That our people are eminently social, the frequent public gatherings here and at Topeka will bear witness. A person coming in to mingle in the scene would never realize he was in a newly settled country, or in a town scarcely a year old.[17]

territory to have been settled for political reasons, it would be the only territory with two governors, two legislatures, two constitutions, and two court systems.

Shortly after the October 23 Free State convention was held, the proslavery legislature met. Unwilling and unable to ignore events in Topeka, Governor Shannon addressed the representatives in the opening session, calling the Topeka meeting treasonable. But if that was the route that the Free Staters wanted to take, Shannon said, two could play that game. He wanted proslavery forces to form one more party in Kansas, a Law and Order party, that would enforce the laws that the legislature had passed. The legislature and numerous volunteers were happy to grant Shannon his wish.

A convention to organize the Law and Order party was set for November 14. To gain as many members as possible, the convention was highly publicized. Announcements appeared throughout the territory and the border country of Missouri, tacked to walls in saloons, nailed on buildings in every city and village, and published in every proslavery newspaper:

Grand Mass Convention at Leavenworth City Nov. 14th, '55

The law-abiding citizens of Kansas Territory, without distinction of party, will hold a grand mass convention, at Leavenworth, on November 14th. Let there be a grand rally of the law and order citizens of the territory. Friends of the constitution and laws, turn out, appoint delegates from every neighborhood, and come yourselves and show that there is a grand and glorious party in the territory, who are determined to stand by the constituted authorities of the land. Let come what will, show that you are determined to rally around the bulwarks of the constitution, and maintain the laws. Let every county in the territory be fully represented.[18]

Armed confrontation was now closer than ever.

Chapter Six

WAR ON THE WAKARUSA

Hostilities between proslavery and antislavery forces increased throughout November 1855. Although several confrontations, mostly over land, ended in violence, it was the death of Charles Dow that got the most attention and had the most frightening results.

Disputes over land claims between proslavery and free soil advocates were common in Kansas, in large part because the Missourians who first marched into the territory to claim it did little more than announce that they owned the land, leaving few if any records and no permanent dwellings. Later, when free soilers arrived and began to build on some of these sites, border ruffians tried to assert their rather shaky rights.

Twelve miles south of Lawrence lay a prime piece of property, a heavily wooded area known as Hickory Point. Free soiler Jacob Branson had settled there, and believing that an adjoining piece of property had not been staked out, he had encouraged a friend, Charles Dow, to claim the land. However, three proslavery supporters in the area, Franklin Coleman, Josiah Hargis, and Harrison Buckley, had refused

Samuel Jones was an ardent proslavery supporter. As sheriff, he attempted to enforce the laws passed by the proslavery legislature in Kansas Territory. Courtesy of the Kansas State Historical Society, Topeka, Kansas

to recognize Dow's claim. In fact, the three men had repeatedly harassed Dow to try to drive him away.

On November 21, Dow met up with Coleman, Hargis, and Buckley at the blacksmith shop in Lawrence. Angry words were exchanged, and Dow's life was threatened. When Dow left the shop, the proslavery men followed him home, and from a distance of about forty yards, Coleman fired at Dow as he dismounted. As Dow spun around and begged for his life, Coleman shot him in the chest. According to one witness, the proslavery men then gathered around the corpse, rejoicing in what Coleman had done.

Sheriff Samuel Jones, a proslavery supporter who lived in Westport, Missouri, and who was responsible for enforcing the law in and around Lawrence, made no effort to arrest Coleman, so Jacob

Branson, along with members of a newly organized Free State militia, decided to take the law into their own hands. Branson questioned Buckley and Hargis, both of whom insisted that Coleman had fired in self-defense. Branson challenged the witnesses' version of events and told them that they ought to reconsider their testimony. He would be back in a few days to talk to them again, he said matter-of-factly, and next time he wanted to hear the truth.

Branson frightened Buckley and Hargis. As soon as the militia was out of sight, the two witnesses moved their families to safety in Missouri and then joined Coleman at the Shawnee Mission, where he had sought refuge.

When Branson and the militiamen returned and realized that the witnesses had fled, the militia's mood turned ugly. Some of the men threatened to set the witnesses' homesteads on fire, but Branson forbade it. Even so, later that evening, someone burned Buckley's and Hargis's cabins and outbuildings to the ground.

Now Sheriff Jones took action. He got a warrant for Branson's arrest, swore in a small posse, and arrested Branson about 2:00 a.m. on November 27.

Word about the arrest spread quickly that night, and fifteen of Branson's militiamen decided to rescue their leader. Believing—correctly—that Branson was being taken to Lecompton, now the proslavery capital, the men rushed toward a narrow bridge about five miles from Lawrence that Jones, his posse, and Branson would have to cross. Branson's friends were more than a bit nervous as they waited. The militiamen were prepared for nothing less than a showdown, a shootout if necessary, and who knew what the repercussions of such action might be?

When Jones and his prisoner arrived around 4:00 a.m., the militiamen came out from their hiding places and, waving their weapons high in the air, told the sheriff and his posse to halt. Jacob Branson, and only Branson, the men said, was to continue across the bridge. Sheriff Jones threatened to shoot Branson if he moved forward, and the militiamen threatened to kill Jones, whom they thoroughly detested, and the posse, which they didn't like much better, if Branson was harmed. So for what seemed like an eternity, no one stirred.

Finally, Branson announced that he was coming toward the militiamen, and as the rescuers held their breath, he did so without a shot being fired. Neither Jones nor any member of his posse dared shoot Branson in the back, especially with so many witnesses. Besides, as Jones later explained, the posse was well aware that the militiamen meant business. They were big, mean, and so heavily armed, Jones recalled, that they could barely move under the weight of their guns, swords, and ammunition pouches.

Jones and his men had been outmaneuvered, which should have upset them. Instead, they were jubilant. Now they had proof that law and order had broken down in the territory. They saw it as an excuse to attack Free Staters, and perhaps even to level the town of Lawrence. They had long been eager to do this, in order to gain the upper hand.

Jones began his campaign to bring the Free Staters into line by telegraphing Governor Shannon. "You may consider," Jones said, "an open rebellion as having already commenced, and I call upon you for three thousand men to carry out the laws."[19]

Shannon was stunned. Even though he had openly sided with proslavery forces, he was not especially eager to support them if it meant war in Kansas. Besides, where was he going to get three thousand men? Local proslavery forces could supply but a few hundred volunteers, far short of what Jones thought he needed. So Shannon telegraphed President Pierce for authority to call out the First Cavalry at Fort Leavenworth, a federal force, which was under the command of Colonel E.V. Sumner.

Sheriff Jones knew that neither the Kansas volunteers nor the federal troops at Fort Leavenworth could provide three thousand soldiers, so while Shannon rounded up as many men as he could, Jones turned to Missourians for help. Jones and Atchison, by this time a former senator, after losing his last campaign, appealed to the Blue Lodges, border ruffians, and each and every able-bodied potential volunteer for duty in Kansas. Atchison announced that not only could volunteers hope to destroy their enemies, they could expect $1 a day *and* a land grant in Kansas when the dust settled. Once again, notices were posted everywhere.

To Arms! To Arms!

It is expected that every lover of Law and Order will rally at Leavenworth on Saturday, December 1, 1855, prepared to march at once to the scene of the rebellion, to put down the outlaws of Douglas county, who are committing depredation upon persons and property, burning down houses and declaring open hostility to the laws, and have forcibly rescued a prisoner from the Sheriff. Come one, come all! The outlaws, it is said, are armed to the teeth, and number 1,000 men. Every man should bring his rifle and ammunition, and it would be well to bring two or three day's provision. Every man to his post, and to his duty.

MANY CITIZENS [20]

The advertising campaign paid off. Jones raised more than fifteen hundred men who formed what was called the Border Army. Most of these men camped and trained near the Wakarusa River near Franklin; the rest pitched their tents in Lecompton. By December 5, Jones was ready to enter Lawrence and Governor Shannon was beside himself.

Antislavery leaders in Lawrence were as upset and apprehensive as Shannon, and they had been in this frame of mind since November 27, when Jacob Branson had returned to Lawrence surrounded by his rescuers. Believing that Jones would come looking for Branson and probably destroy the town in the process, these leaders had formed the Committee of Safety. Charles Robinson had been elected to take

In this 1856 photo, Free Staters stand beside one of their cannons, an invaluable weapon during the civil war in Kansas. Courtesy of the Kansas State Historical Society, Topeka, Kansas

command of the situation and James Lane had been chosen second-in-command.

Robinson and the committee had immediately sought some way to defuse the situation. They had taken Branson and his rescuers out of town so that the Border Army would have no excuse to enter Lawrence. Next, Robinson had begun to prepare a formal statement, which was to be sent to the governor, insisting that the rescue of Branson was the work of several individuals, not the townspeople. The people of Lawrence, Robinson said, knew nothing about the militia's plans or deeds, and therefore they should not be punished.

While Robinson had worked on his statement, Lane had been very busy, using his military experience to oversee the building of four earth-and-wood forts, which were designed to protect the town. These forts were well made, providing great security to the men inside, who would be able to claim many victims among the attackers. In addition, the free soilers had somehow managed to get their hands on a cannon. Lane had put this in plain sight to alert the enemy to the fact that the townspeople had weapons of great firepower. As Law and Order supporters had already observed, the townspeople also had many Sharpe's rifles, one of the finest weapons available at the time. In short, Lawrencians were not to be underestimated.

Lane had also started to train volunteers, many of whom spent a good part of each day marching and target shooting. Those who could not fight had been instructed on how best to find safety. Hannah Ropes, who had been in the territory for only two months, was given very specific directions, as were many other women. "My orders are," she wrote to her mother, "if fire-arms sound like battle, to place Alice [her daughter] and myself as near the floor as possible, and be well covered with blankets."[21]

Citizens had also been told to spring into action at the least sign of trouble, and this included hearing strange noises. Hannah remarked that this had sometimes led to humorous incidents.

> I, hardly daring to close my eyes, at last, half asleep, hearing the most fiendish outcry ever borne upon the moon-lit night air, call aloud, "Wake up, quickly! There is trouble of some kind, for nothing but a Missourian could utter such sounds this side of [hell]!" [All in] the cabin [are] astir in an instant, only to laugh at me, because the unearthly sounds are only those of a party of wolves taking a survey of the city at midnight.[22]

Although precautions were being taken, at first most Lawrencians refused to believe that they were in any danger. Even Sara Robinson, who had more knowledge of what was happening than most citizens, scoffed at the idea. On November 28, Sara wrote:

It is rumored that a large force is gathering at Franklin, also another at Lecompton, fourteen miles above here. We do not credit such reports. Whom will they fight, if they come? Will they dare, in this nineteenth century, in this boasted land of freedom, to make a raid upon us, crying, "Extermination, and no quarter!" A wholesome fear of consequences to themselves will prevent this. There will, probably, be a good deal of useless bravado, and they will strive to place us, if possible, in a wrong position before the world.[23]

But as the number of volunteers in the Border Army had grown, even Sara had to admit that Lawrence was in trouble, and by December 1, her mood was somber at best.

Dec. 1st.—Saturday night has come again, bringing the close of another week—a week of anxiety to the leaders here, upon whom the responsibility of our safety rests. Messengers have been sent to the other settlements, at different times, notifying them of the threatened attack, with the desire that they hold themselves in readiness to come to our aid at a moment's notice.

Last night, at midnight, a friendly band of armed men came in from Ottawa Creek, having heard of the invasion. With flag flying, a company of mounted riflemen have come in from Palmyra, also. The Indians, both Shawnees and Delawares, have offered their warriors for our defense. While we would not accept aid from the Indians, knowing that it would furnish a pretext to the government for their extermination, their friendly feelings will go far towards sustaining the courage of any who might falter.[24]

The following week, the number of border ruffians and scouts trying to get a closer look at their enemies had increased dramatically. Eager for battle, ruffians had fired a few shots at the men building forts. Those in Lawrence, however, had held their fire. No one wanted to give the Border Army any reason to invade.

Governor Wilson Shannon, the second governor of Kansas Territory, failed to stop the fighting between proslavery and antislavery forces. Courtesy of the Kansas State Historical Society, Topeka, Kansas

Governor Wilson Shannon

By mid-week, when Sheriff Jones had planned to attack, tension inside the town had become almost unbearable. Hannah Ropes said:

> *Dec. 5th.*—Mother of mine, I can hardly settle down to the details of our own matters. Everything over the town, and every rumor borne in to us from outside of it, is more and more dark and fearful. We now have an armed force of five hundred men, who are under the command of Dr. Robinson . . . and Colonel Lane, both of whom have had experience in actual battle in Mexico and California. Out of my south window I can see them drilling. . . . We draw close to the window as the soldiers pass by. . . . But what a long line of men it is! Not noisy; and there is no rabble of boys at the roadsides. Boys there are in the ranks; but the soberness of

manhood is upon them, and the determination of "Seventy-six" in their step. The blood warms in my veins as I look. [25]

While the two sides continued to make their preparations, Governor Shannon tried to prevent violence. He began by visiting the Border Army near the Wakarusa River on December 6. He quickly realized that these men wanted nothing less than all-out war. One of the ruffians told a shocked Shannon, "We mean to have Kansas. And we are going to have it, if we have to wade through blood to our knees to get it."[26]

Shannon believed that the men leading the army were not only of the same opinion, they were barely able to keep the volunteers under control. How much longer, Shannon wondered, before these men would simply form a mob and attack the town? Now Shannon was more eager than ever to have help from the federal troops at Fort Leavenworth. He hoped they would act as a restraining force. But every appeal for troops was rejected. The commander at the fort would not act without orders from Washington, and those orders were slow in coming. Shannon finally appealed successfully to David Atchison to keep the Border Army in camp.

The next day, Governor Shannon, with several representatives from the proslavery forces, visited Lawrence, where they met with members of the Committee of Safety at the Free State Hotel, the committee's headquarters. The hotel was also serving as a place of mourning. The night before, Thomas Barber, a volunteer with Lane's army, had left Lawrence to go home to cut wood for his wife and parents. Barber, who was with several other Free Staters, had been stopped by a dozen ruffians. An argument ensued, and Barber was shot dead. His body was then brought to the hotel for a public viewing. Now as Shannon made his way to the meeting room, he was forced to pass Barber's body, his grieving widow, and his enraged friends.

Shannon realized that the townspeople were in no mood to compromise, let alone surrender, but he asked them to give up their weapons anyway. Committee members insisted that the rifles were private property and that Shannon had no right to ask citizens for their belongings. Besides, committee members pointed out, those rifles were their only hope of protection against those they considered to be nothing less than cold-blooded murderers. Look at what they did to Barber! they shouted. Who would protect them if they surrendered their guns? Sheriff Jones?

Disheartened and sick with worry, Shannon left Lawrence to seek out Atchison once more. The governor now tried to convince Atchison that an attack on Lawrence was pure folly. Shannon argued that fifteen hundred heavily armed men charging into a town of men, women, and children to arrest outlaws who were not there would bring condemnation upon the ruffians and contempt for their cause. The Border Army would suffer heavy casualties, Shannon added, for the Lawrencians were in a fighting mood since the death of Barber. It was better, the governor said, to disperse the army.

These were not the words that Atchison wanted to hear, but he eventually agreed with Shannon. An invasion would be the wrong move. He then addressed his restless men. "Boys, we cannot fight now. The position the Lawrence people have taken is such that it would not do to make an attack upon it. . . . But boys, we will fight some time, by God!"[27] Unwilling to simply walk away and hoping that Atchison might change his mind, the vast majority of ruffians remained in camp.

Knowing full well that until the Border Army went home, he had only gained time, Shannon returned to Lawrence the following day, December 8, to hammer out an agreement. Robinson and his committee repeated their original position: They were not responsible for what had happened and they would not surrender their weapons. But, in the interest of peace, they would agree to recognize "proper authority."

Shannon was elated. He had, he thought, resolved the crisis, for the committee's concession would end the conflict. The proslavery government would finally be recognized and accepted by the Free Staters. But Shannon had been duped by the committee.

How cleverly Shannon had been deceived became clear when the agreement was presented to the townspeople. John Brown, who was part of Lane's volunteer army, flew into a rage when the statement about respecting "proper authority" was read. Brown stood up, shook his fists at the committee members, and shouted that he would *never* recognize "proper authority," believing, as did Shannon, that the members were referring to the governor and the bogus legislature. When committee members assured him that the phrase was meant to be vague and misleading—the committee meant federal officials, not anyone in the territory— Brown refused to believe them, storming out of the meeting to show his disgust.

While Brown made his way home that night, the Border Army began to break up. The Lawrencians' supposed concession had made an attack impossible. Besides, the disgruntled ruffians had a new enemy to face. Late that afternoon, a cold front and gale-force winds had begun to sweep down from the north, turning rain into driving pellets of sleet that stung and even cut exposed flesh. Later, the winds became so intense that the campfires the men were using to warm themselves had to be put out when embers whipped about by gusts of wind set tents and clothing on fire. The thought of a warm cabin with a blazing fire was now too much to resist, and one by one, the bitterly disappointed men began to pack up their weapons and gear and head for home. Meanwhile, Lawrencians, realizing what a powerful ally the cold was, uttered a simple prayer. "Oh, Lord, send it a little colder."[28]

Chapter Seven
A New Free State?

Governor Shannon's belief that the Free Staters had finally accepted the territory's proslavery government was dashed within a week. On December 15, to Shannon's utter dismay, party leaders rolled up their sleeves and set up polling booths so Kansans could vote on the Free State constitution.

Even though there were some violent incidents between Free Staters and their proslavery opponents on election day, most opponents chose to ignore the election. Many proslavery supporters considered the election illegal. Besides, since the first storm had arrived on December 8, the weather had been getting worse by the day, making it too miserable for Missourians, even the toughest of the ruffians, to invade Kansas again. On Christmas Eve, December 24, Sara Robinson noted in her journal, "Still snowing, and the weather terribly severe. The thermometer seventeen degrees below zero, wind is blowing, and the snow drifting into all imaginable shapes. . . . To face a Missouri mob is nothing to facing these winds which sweep over the prairies."[29]

Without interference, an overwhelming number of Free State voters approved the constitution their delegates had drafted.

Emboldened by their success, Free Staters marched to the polls again on January 15, 1856, this time to elect officers for their new government. These included a governor (Dr. Charles Robinson), lieutenant governor, treasurer, secretary, nineteen senators, and fifty-six representatives. A swearing-in session, when the new government would officially begin to function, was set for March 4.

Meanwhile, both sides, determined to win, looked for support not only in Kansas but in America in general. Newspaper editors led the fight for public opinion, reporting their enemies' activities in the most sensational way possible. In addition, rumors were eagerly passed along as were exaggerated accounts of assaults and attacks. Eventually some of these stories were reprinted in national newspapers.

The passionate accounts deeply upset Douglas Brewerton, a reporter from New York. "Kansas Territory," he said, "has . . . been the theatre of too many windy battles, in which words—words—words—words—bad words—harsh words—devilish words—have been rattled down like hail-stones, night after night, and day after day, by interested *talkers* upon either side, who didn't care a brass farthing [about] the true interests of the people."[30] Despite Brewerton's disgust, the lurid accounts continued, gaining supporters for each side every day.

Free Staters and proslavery supporters also reached out to powerful individuals outside the territory for help. For example, Free State party leaders asked settlers to write to any congressmen they knew personally, hoping to persuade senators and representatives to intervene in the struggle in Kansas.

One of the first settlers involved in a letter-writing campaign was Hannah Ropes, whose friends included Senator Charles Sumner from Massachusetts, her home state. She sent Sumner a lengthy letter just before the Border Army gathered outside Lawrence. She said, in part:

> Here in Lawrence, no week has ever passed without . . . insult
> thrown at our people by our nearest neighbors, the Missourians.
> We never ride, even within our own territory, and meet them, but
> our ears are pained with words too wicked to repeat. And they

shoot at defenceless people with as much cool indifference as they would at partridges or prairie chickens.

My poor woman's head does not pretend to sift or unravel this state of things. I am only [aware] of the present sad and dangerous conditions in which, as a town, we find ourselves. You who are wise and benevolent should be able to help us who are so defenceless. . . .

It gives me pleasure to affirm that I have known of no outrage . . . on the part of [the] hard-struggling [emigrants]. I can but believe [our problems] to be wholly the result of bitter opposition to Eastern people . . . strong enough to lead Missouri to put forth her mean and treacherous hand, with the will to tear up by the roots every settlement where the [S]outhern mark is not stamped upon its inhabitants. O, men of Congress! where is the use of your assembling together, if not for the good of those who are in need of your aid? . . . Long before this reaches you, other victims will sleep their last sleep. Our houses are no protection. There is hardly a cabin which a strong man could not tear down. Let me add . . . that I am proud of Kansas and Kansas men and women [and their] energy, courage, good judgment, and noble magnanimity shown in these nights and days of danger. . . .[31]

H.A.R.

While Hannah pleaded with Senator Sumner, on the opposite side of the conflict David Atchison contacted Southern leaders for help:

We are in a constant state of excitement here. . . . The very air is full of rumors. We wish to keep ourselves right before the world, [but] we are provoked and aggravated beyond sufferance. Our persons and property are not for a moment safe; and yet are forbid, by the respect we owe our friends elsewhere, by respect for the cause in which we are engaged, to forbear. This state of things cannot last. Let your young men come forth to Missouri and Kansas. Let them come well armed, with money enough to support them for twelve months, and determined to see this thing out! . . . The more the better.

I do not see how we are to avoid civil war; come it will. . . . We are arming and preparing for it. Indeed, we of the border counties are prepared. We must have the support of the South. We are fighting the battles of the South. Our institutions are at stake. . . . We want men, armed men. We want money—not for ourselves, but to support our friends who may come from a distance.

Yours truly,
D.R. Atchison

P.S. . . . I was a peace-maker in the difficulty lately settled by Gov. Shannon. I counseled the "ruffians" to forbearance, but I will never again counsel peace. D.R.A.[32]

Southerners responded generously to Atchison's call. In Alabama, Major Jefferson Buford sold forty slaves and used the proceeds to raise a small army, three hundred men in all. Colonel Zachabod Jackson from Georgia and Colonel Warren D. Wilkes of South Carolina also recruited men for the cause and then led them to Kansas. State legislatures in Georgia and Alabama introduced bills to tax slaveholders and use the proceeds to either arm more men or send more emigrants.

While some men and women were writing letters, others were making pleas in person. Sam Wood, the leader of Branson's rescue party, gave speeches to various antislavery groups in the North after being hustled out of Lawrence. He asked these groups to send money, guns, and men. Six members from the Committee of Safety, including James Lane, also took to the speaking circuit in early January 1856, seeking men and munitions.

These pleas were very effective. On January 24, Sara Robinson noted in her journal, "A half ton of lead, and nearly as much powder, arrived to-day. Other teams, loaded with the same needful, are on the way. Provisions, too, are fast coming in, and we will soon be able to stand quite a siege."[33]

The Election of 1856

The Election of 1856

Millard Fillmore. Courtesy of the Dover Pictorial
Archives

Millard Fillmore

One of the results of the fight over slavery in Kansas was the formation of the Republican party in 1854. Although members had many issues they wanted to put before the voters, it was the Republicans' opposition to any expansion of slavery that made the party unique, drawing thousands of free-soil Democrats into its ranks as well as Northern members of the Whig party,

James Buchanan. Courtesy of the Dover Pictorial
Archives

James Buchanan

which included some of the wealthiest men in the country
and was, like the Democratic party, torn asunder by the issue
of slavery.

After successfully fielding candidates on the local level,
Republicans decided to run a candidate in the 1856 presidential election. They chose John C. Frémont, a military hero from
the Mexican War. Frémont's campaign slogan was, "Free Soil,
Free Speech, Free Men, Frémont!"

President Pierce hoped that the Democrats would
renominate him, but party leaders chose James Buchanan
instead. They believed that Pierce had alienated too many
Northern Democrats with his handling of events in Kansas,

John Charles Frémont. Courtesy of the Dover
Pictorial Archives

John Charles Frémont

driving members into the ranks of the Republican party, which
was a political sin. Besides an impressive background in the
U.S. House of Representatives and the Senate, and as President
Polk's secretary of state, Buchanan's main asset was his absence
from the country while Kansas bled. He had been serving as an
ambassador to England then, and had not been tainted by
events in the territory. Also, Buchanan was opposed to slavery
on moral grounds, which leaders thought would win votes in
the North, but committed to protecting slavery where it exist-
ed, which would win votes in the South.

A third party, a mix of two political groups, the rest of the
Whigs and the Know-Nothings, so called because members,

sworn to secrecy, replied that they knew nothing when asked about the party's operations, called itself the American party. It nominated former President Millard Fillmore. He avoided the slavery issue altogether.

On election day, voters cast almost four million ballots. This was an especially large turnout. Democrat Buchanan won 45 percent of the popular vote, the vast majority of which came from the South. Frémont claimed 33 percent of the ballots, carrying eleven of sixteen Northern states. This was a stunning accomplishment for a party that was but a few years old. The American party garnered 22 percent of the popular vote, most of which came from states such as Maryland that had slaves as well as strong economic ties to the North. These border states would be the most likely battleground in the event of a civil war. The results indicated a serious split in the country that became more evident in the following years. In the next presidential election in 1860, when the issue of slavery was even more pronounced, Republican candidate Abraham Lincoln would not receive a *single* vote in the South.

While Kansans were preparing for civil war, President Pierce was worrying about the next presidential election, which was to be held in the fall of 1856. No matter what stand he took on Kansas, his chances of serving a second term were in jeopardy. The fight over slavery in the territory had pitted Northern and Southern Democrats against each other more violently than ever before, causing a major rift in his party. Disgusted with events in Kansas and the role some party leaders were playing in the struggle, free-soil Democrats were actually threatening to abandon the party, thereby reducing the number of Democratic voters in the fall. But if he tried to accommodate the free soilers, he was certain to lose the support of many—if not all—Southern Democrats.

Pierce's secretary of war was Jefferson Davis, who in five short years would become the president of the Confederacy. He convinced Pierce that the only way to end the struggle in Kansas and to keep his party together was to admit the territory as a state as soon as possible, thereby ending the ongoing debate once and for all. So on January 24, Pierce asked Congress to pass an enabling act that would grant Kansans the right to apply for statehood. He also endorsed the proslavery legislature and condemned the Free State party calling its actions "treasonable."

How treasonable the actions of the Free Staters were in Pierce's eyes became very clear a few days later. Leaders of the Free State party, trying every means possible to safeguard their people, had sent a letter to Pierce, requesting protection from an anticipated attack in the spring from the Border Army:

Lawrence, K.T., January 21, 1856

Hon. Franklin Pierce, President of the United States:

Sir—We have authentic information that an overwhelming force of the citizens of Missouri are organized on the Border, amply supplied with artillery, for the avowed purpose of invading the Territory, demolishing our towns and butchering our unoffending Free-state citizens. We respectfully demand, on behalf of the citizens of Kansas, that the Commandant of the U.S. troops in this vicinity be instructed to interfere to prevent such an inhuman outrage.

Respectfully,

J. H. Lane, *Chairman of Executive Committee of Kansas Territory*

C. Robinson, *Chairman of Executive Committee of Safety*

J.K. Goodin, *Secretary of Executive Committee of Kansas Territory*

Geo. W. Deitzler, *Secretary of Executive Committee of Safety.* [34]

Pierce agreed that outside forces, such as the Missourians, had no place in Kansas, so he promised to provide protection from such men if an invasion took place. However, he thundered, by refusing to accept the proslavery legislature and obey the governors he had sent, Free Staters had broken the law. If local leaders such as Sheriff Jones marched into Lawrence to enforce legislation, Pierce would not interfere. And if Jones decided that federal troops were needed to serve warrants, he would order soldiers to do so. This announcement would have disastrous results in the territory.

Chapter Eight
THE PRICE OF TREASON

Although President Pierce was eager to admit Kansas as a state, congressmen were hesitant to even discuss the issue, fearing correctly that it would tear the legislature apart. Senators and representatives alike had long hoped and prayed that they would never have to become involved in events in Kansas again after they had passed the Kansas-Nebraska Act. Now they found themselves being drawn into the struggle. Northern and Southern congressmen accused the other side of fraud and manipulation. Believing that they could right a wrong, both antislavery and proslavery men wanted an enabling act that favored their side. So for months, the legislators squabbled among themselves, repeatedly introducing and rejecting bills.

The debate over Kansas became even more complicated when James Lane, on behalf of the Free State legislature, arrived in Washington, D.C., in early March with a petition for statehood in his hand and a constitution tucked under his arm. Startled congressmen, who had anticipated but one application and who were well aware that the proslavery legislature also planned to apply for statehood, suddenly realized that they would have two petitions. Now Congress would be forced to decide which application to accept, thereby determining whether Kansas would be free or slave.

But Lane, much to Congress's relief, inadvertently gave it two excuses to postpone action. First of all, every name listed on the petition was in the same handwriting, a fact Senator Stephen A. Douglas was quick to point out. When Lane explained that the original had been so badly damaged that he had asked his secretary to copy it, more than a few senators laughed aloud.

Then congressmen looked at the Free State constitution, which would have to be approved before the territory could become a state. This document was a tattered, dirty mess. Parts were written in pencil, erasures were common, and whole sections had been crossed out, making the document difficult to interpret. Congressmen glanced at the papers and then sneered at Lane. Why Lane made such a sloppy presentation is unclear. Perhaps he believed that the proslavery legislature's constitution was quick in coming and that he had to be first, giving him no time to rewrite it before turning it over to a congressional committee. But because the document was so confusing, congressmen were hesitant to even examine it. Instead, they delayed as long as possible.

Although representatives and senators knew that they had bought themselves a little time by questioning Lane's documents, they also knew that they could not ignore the issue of statehood for long. But in order to decide how best to proceed, they needed more information. So the House of Representatives, resisting irate proslavery supporters who insisted that Kansans work out their own problems, decided to hold an investigation.

On March 19, the House chose John Sherman from Ohio and William Howard from Michigan, both of whom were free soilers, and Mordecai Oliver from Missouri, a proslavery Democrat, to go to Kansas to gather information. The three men arrived in Lecompton on April 17. They announced that statements would be taken in Lecompton, Lawrence, Tecumseh, and Leavenworth over the coming weeks. Kansans who had information about the elections and events in the territory were asked to come forward, and come forward they did.

Eventually the witnesses' testimony would fill more than one thousand pages. The stories that the men and women told convinced the two Northern representatives that voter fraud had been so commonplace that the results should not be honored. On the other hand, other witnesses persuaded Representative Oliver that all was well in Kansas. In other words, the investigation solved nothing.

While the representatives gathered their information, Sheriff Jones, who had had arrest warrants for members of Branson's rescue party for months, was biding his time, waiting for Sam Wood to return to the territory. When proslavery supporters finally spotted Wood in Lawrence, Jones was more than ready for action.

On April 19, the sheriff galloped into town to round up his prisoners. As luck would have it, he quickly spotted Wood on the street, where he confronted him and ordered him to surrender. Wood refused and started to walk away. Townspeople then surrounded Jones to give Wood time to escape. They pushed the sheriff to-and-fro, and in the process, removed his gun. Outmaneuvered and more than a little embarrassed, Jones left Lawrence shortly after.

Sheriff Jones wasn't about to give up though. On Sunday morning, April 20, he returned with four deputies and warrants for the arrest of some of the men who had surrounded him the day before. The streets were filled with people on their way to church. Intent upon attending services and eager to avoid trouble, the men and women ignored Jones. Many even refused to look at him when he spoke to them and asked the whereabouts of the men he sought. As soon as the churchgoers had cleared the streets, an armed group of men gathered around the sheriff to heckle him. Sam Tappan, one of the men in the Branson rescue party, was in this group, and Jones recognized him. As the sheriff moved toward Tappan, a scuffle broke out, and Jones was punched in the mouth. Humiliated and outnumbered once again, he and his deputies rode out of town as the crowd hooted and howled.

Still refusing to give up, Jones turned to Colonel Sumner at Fort Leavenworth for the help that President Pierce had promised in January. Sumner sent a message to Lawrence warning the townspeople not to interfere with the sheriff's activities. He then ordered an officer and ten men to accompany Jones the next time he served arrest warrants.

The posse arrived in Lawrence on April 23. Although the townspeople jeered Jones and the soldiers, Lawrencians took Sumner's warning seriously, and they did little to interfere with the arrests. As a result, the sheriff managed to take at least six men into custody that day. But his work was not finished—he had forty names on his list now—so after locking his prisoners in a room, he and the soldiers set up tents outside the building for the night. While Jones sat in his tent, someone shot him in the back.

As Jones thrashed about in agony, Lawrencians didn't know whether to cheer or cry. It was no secret that most of them hated the sheriff. They were well aware, though, that because Jones had been shot in Lawrence—in the back, yet—the town once again faced possible invasion and reprisal.

Leaders of the Committee of Safety immediately swung into action, and they publicly disavowed any knowledge of the shooting. One of the leaders even offered a reward for the capture of the assailant. Meanwhile, townspeople did their best to comfort Jones, whose wound, although serious, was not mortal.

Free Staters may have had mixed feelings about the attack on Jones, but proslavery supporters knew only one emotion—outrage. Rumors ran rampant, each new one more shocking than the old, and within hours Jones was declared dead, a murder victim of an incredibly foul assailant who, along with his supporters, deserved the worst punishment possible. John Stringfellow, the editor of the *Squatter Sovereign* wrote: "ABOLITIONISTS IN OPEN REBELLION—SHERIFF JONES MURDERED BY THE TRAITORS. HE MUST BE AVENGED. HIS MURDER SHALL BE AVENGED, if at the sacrifice of every abolitionist in the Territory. . . . We are now in favor of leveling Lawrence, and chastising the Traitors there congregated, should it result in the total destruction of the Union."[35]

While Stringfellow raged, even after he learned that Jones was not dead, the courts became involved. On May 5, a grand jury in a federal district court, comprised only of proslavery advocates, handed down three decisions. First, leaders of the Free State party, including Reeder, Robinson, and Lane, were officially charged with treason. Second, because the *Herald of Freedom* had published information "of the most inflammatory and seditious character, denying the legality of the territorial authorities . . . and demoralizing the popular mind," and the *Kansas Free State* had dared to report the resolutions of a public meeting "in which resistance to the territorial laws even unto blood has been agreed upon"[36] the newspapers should be shut down. And third, because the Free State Hotel had been used for meetings where treasonable acts had been plotted, and could serve as a stronghold against the law, it should be destroyed. The arrests were to be made by U.S. Marshal I.B. Donalson and a posse of his choosing. The shutting down of the presses and the destruction of the hotel were Sheriff Jones's responsibility.

Proslavery supporters cheered the decisions. They now had the backing of a federal court and the support of federal troops to enter Lawrence and enforce the law.

On May 11, Marshal Donalson warned Free State leaders that his assistant, Deputy Marshal Fain, and his posse would be serving the writs, and he hoped that townspeople would be cooperative. To resist, he said, could lead to bloodshed.

Heartsick Free State leaders held a series of meetings to decide what to do. The townspeople could put up a fight, especially if they received help from Free Staters in nearby towns and villages. But to resist federal troops and the authority they represented was downright dangerous. Not only could resistance result in even more destruction and the loss of life, fighting federal authorities would cost them dearly in the court of public opinion. Furthermore, emigrant society leaders in Massachusetts now insisted that Lawrencians cooperate in order to save the town and promote the society's cause. This was a great opportunity to win a moral victory, society leaders said. Imagine the level of indignation across the country when the public learns that a posse invaded Lawrence to do its worst to unarmed men, women, and children!

After much hand-wringing, Lawrencians finally agreed to put aside their arms and accept the onslaught. Most party leaders, in order to avoid arrest, disguised themselves and prepared to leave the territory. Despite their best efforts, several, including Dr. Robinson, were captured.

For almost two weeks, Missourians and their newly acquired recruits from Alabama and Georgia had been gathering outside Lawrence, waiting for action. They routinely stopped Free Staters entering or leaving town, taking their horses and carriages, confiscating their goods, and even assaulting men without provocation. Mobs also robbed homes in the country and seized chickens and cattle when they wanted food. As the numbers of ruffians increased, they formed a ring around Lawrence, moving closer and closer to the town every day, announcing their presence by appearing high on Mt. Oread, a hill, despite its name, just outside of town.

On May 20, the deputy marshal, after stationing more than two hundred men around the town and positioning four cannon pointed at the heart of Lawrence, rode into town with a posse of ten men. After taking several prisoners, he left without incident.

The following morning the deputy returned, again with ten men, arresting as many on his list as he thought possible. The rest, he decided, had either fled town or were so cleverly hidden he couldn't find them. Satisfied that he had done his best, the deputy then returned to Sara Robinson's home, which had been seized by the federal troops to be used as a headquarters, and authorized Sheriff Jones and his posse to enter Lawrence to carry out their orders.

This was the moment that Jones had long awaited. The sheriff gleefully chose a few men to accompany him, and with his head held high, he rode into Lawrence about 3:00 p.m. After announcing to the occupants of the Free State Hotel that they had an hour to evacuate the building, Jones demanded that Lawrencians surrender their cannon and weapons. One of the Free State party leaders led the sheriff to the town's only cannon and a pile of rifles, a small fraction of those hidden in the town, which the leader claimed were the only weapons the party owned. Satisfied that Lawrence was disarmed, Jones rode to Mt. Oread, where the majority of the invaders were stationed.

When the sheriff reached the men, now eight hundred strong, David Atchison was addressing them. Trying to make up for the last gathering around Lawrence, when he counseled peace, his words were especially harsh. He told the men that if they found any woman with a weapon in her hands, they were "to trample her under foot as you would a snake." Then, spotting Jones, Atchison took a deep breath and squared his shoulders. "And now," he said with unmistakable pride, "we will go in with our highly honorable Jones, and test the strength of that damned Free-State Hotel. Be brave, be orderly, and if any man or woman stands in your way, blow them to hell with a chunk of cold lead."[37]

At 4:00 p.m., Jones rode into town again, this time with twenty men. He immediately divided his posse into three groups. One group was sent to the office of the *Herald of Freedom* and a second to the rooms where the *Kansas Free Press* was printed. The writ handed down by the grand jury simply said that the presses were to be stopped. The decision of how to do this was left up to Jones. He chose the most destructive method possible. Under his direction, posse members smashed the presses and threw the pieces into the street. Next, they ransacked the offices. The men forced open desks and filing cabinets and tore records into bits. They destroyed libraries at both sites, carrying some of the books into the streets on the tips of their bayonets. Finally, the men dragged boxes of type to the river and dumped the metal letters and numbers into the water while the editors and reporters looked on helplessly.

The third group was sent to the hotel. Posse members placed kegs of gunpowder inside the building and positioned a cannon in front of the structure to bombard the walls and ignite the powder. It took many shots before the building began to crumble and burn. Jones shouted with joy each time a keg exploded. "This," he said, "is the happiest moment of my life. I determined to make the fanatics bow before me in the dust and kiss the Territorial laws. I have done it,

"The Crime Against Kansas"

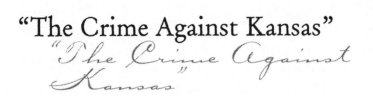

Senator Charles Sumner. Courtesy of the Dover
Pictorial Archives

On May 20, 1856, after enduring heated debates over various bills that would make it possible for Kansans to apply for statehood, Senator Charles Sumner of Massachusetts delivered a controversial speech titled "The Crime Against Kansas," which outraged Southerners and stunned even his staunchest supporters. It wasn't the first time that Sumner, a radical abolitionist, had gotten attention for his fiery speeches, however. After being elected to Congress in 1851, he had taken on the Compromise of 1850, even though it had already passed, attacking the fugitive slave clause with so much vigor and venom that from then on Southern congressmen had nothing but contempt for the senator. Three years later, he attacked the Kansas-Nebraska Act with equal rancor, reaping the wrath of Stephen A. Douglas in the process. So when Sumner took the floor on May 20, senators expected a contentious speech. They did not, however, anticipate the violence that followed.

Sumner, the senator to whom Hannah Ropes had written earlier that year, decried events in Kansas. There he said, "the ballot-box . . . has been plundered . . . and the cry, 'I am an American citizen,' has [had little effect] against outrage of every kind, even upon life itself." Sumner then went on to blame crimes in Kansas on the South's eagerness to have another slave state. "Not in any common lust for power did this uncommon tragedy have its origin," he said. "It may be clearly traced to a depraved longing for a new slave State." Worse yet, Sumner thundered, "When the whole world . . . is rising up to condemn [slavery] here in our Republic, force, ay, sir, FORCE has been openly employed in compelling Kansas to this pollution, and all for the sake of political power." Then he described the enforcers, the border ruffians, as hirelings who had been picked from "drunken spew and vomit."

While senators held their breath, Sumner continued, singling out two members for even harsher words: Stephen A. Douglas, for authoring the Kansas-Nebraska Act that led to the struggle in Kansas, and Andrew Butler, a senator from South Carolina. Butler's crime, in Sumner's eyes, was twofold: supporting slavery and representing South Carolina. Because of its slave trade, Sumner said South Carolina had little of which it could be proud. Sumner then drew an image that was shocking in its day. "[Butler] has chosen a mistress to whom he has made his vows," Sumner said, "and who, though ugly to others, is always lovely to him; though polluted in the sight of the world, is chaste in his sight. I mean the harlot, Slavery."

Wide-eyed senators gasped at the insults. Even so, Sumner continued, pointing out that South Carolina had repeatedly threatened to leave the Union whenever slavery was imperiled. Sumner called the very mention of secession dangerous and Butler, one of its leading spokesman, "one of the maddest zealots" in the South.[38]

Two days later, while Sumner was writing at his desk in the Senate, Representative Preston Brooks, a nephew of Senator Butler and a South Carolinian, attacked and beat Sumner viciously with a cane. Explaining his actions later, Brooks said, "I felt it my duty to relieve Butler and avenge the insult to my State. . . . To punish an insulting inferior one used not a pistol or sword but a cane or horsewhip. . . . Every lick went where I intended. . . . I wore my cane out completely."[39] Sumner was so disabled by the blows, thirty in all, that he would not be able to return to the Senate for more than three years.

The attack on Sumner stunned Americans. Now, not only had the controversy over Kansas torn asunder the Democratic party, pitting Northerners against Southerners, the violence that afflicted settlers in Kansas had actually spread into Congress itself. As a result, before entering the Senate or the House of Representatives, congressmen armed themselves with handguns and Bowie knives. Few were willing to discuss the issue of slavery in Kansas, even in Congress, without protection.

by God, I have done it!"[40] By nightfall, the hotel was little more than a smoldering ruin.

Once the presses and hotel were destroyed, Jones had completed his official duties, so he dismissed his posse. But instead of riding out of town, posse members, joined by hundreds of ruffians who had been celebrating and drinking on Mt. Oread, took advantage of the unarmed citizens, looting Lawrence and setting several homes on fire, including Sara Robinson's.

Sara noted in her journal:

[The dismissal] was the signal for a general plunder of private houses, and as the drunken gang rushed from place to place, they took anything of value upon which their eyes fell. They rifled trunks, taking letters, money, drafts, apparel, both ladies' and gentlemen's, and destroyed anything that would break, even to daguerreotypes and children's toys. Before the day was over, many of the citizens recognized, upon the before ragged persons of the militia, a hat, coat, vest, or pair of pantaloons, to which they had had previous titles, with some of the heavy curtain-cords and tassels, taken from the hotel, worn around them in lieu of sashes; and, with expensive silk or satin dresses on their arms, they marched about, evidently elated with their transformation. In many houses whatever [homeowners] left was mutilated and defaced, and the people, on returning to their homes, found only a wreck of those things which had [given them] comfort. [41]

As the townspeople surveyed the scene and Sara watched her home burn, Lawrencians, weary and worn with care, pondered the cost of treason. It was, they decided, high indeed

Chapter Nine

REIGN OF TERROR

T he attack on Lawrence on May 21, 1856, was a turning
point in the fight over slavery in Kansas. Until then, the
majority of Free Staters had chosen the paths of self-
defense or nonresistance, in part to garner support from the
American public, which settlers believed they needed in
order to make Kansas a free state. Now, with one of their
towns in ruins, their leaders on the run or imprisoned, and
their future bleak at best, many Free Staters changed their
minds. Public support be damned! they shouted. It was time
for all-out war!

John Brown had been advocating such a war since he
had entered the territory in early 1856. In fact, Brown had
become so determined to fight that he had refused to
accept the Committee of Safety's decision not to resist
Jones and his posse. When the invaders had charged into
Lawrence, Brown had been on his way to round up volunteers to defend the town even if the Lawrencians wouldn't
do so.

After the attack on Lawrence, Brown's hatred of his
rivals knew no bounds. He couldn't punish the entire posse,
but he could lash out at proslavery supporters and make

examples of them. The results were the Pottawatomie Creek massacres of May 24 to 25, 1856, in which five proslavery settlers were
slaughtered.

After the massacres, enraged proslavery supporters scoured the
countryside for Brown. One of them was Henry Clay Pate, who had
about sixty men in his posse. Upon arriving at the Brown homestead,
Pate seized the only Browns he could find, John, Jr. and Jason, refusing to believe that the abolitionist's sons had not participated in the
massacres. Shortly after, Pate ran into federal soldiers, who after hearing rumors that Lawrencians were arming themselves, were trying to
keep the proslavery forces and the Free Staters from killing each
other. The soldiers took the prisoners from the posse and told Pate's
men to disband.

But Pate wasn't about to go home. As soon as the soldiers were out
of sight, he and his posse resumed their search. As they did so, the men
plundered nearby Palmyra, seizing horses for the hunt and weapons for
the kill.

Brown was well hidden and protected by local sympathizers,
many of whom considered the abolitionist a hero. As a result, finding
Brown wasn't as easy as Pate thought it would be. So on June 1, he
divided his men into several scouting groups to try to cover as much
ground as possible. One of these groups rode into Prairie City. A
shootout between Pate's men and some local citizens took place, even
though it was Sunday morning and the citizens were in church when
the posse arrived. One parishioner recalled:

> [D]uring the course of [the] sermon an excitement in the congre-
> gation suddenly broke out. Many men jumped up and ran for
> their guns which they had deposited in the corner as they came in.
> . . . [O]n going to the door I saw six men riding up, armed and in
> line. . . . [W]hen the men rushed out with their guns cocked, four
> of these men surrendered, but two in the rear turned and fled as
> fast as their horses could run, with bullets from our churchmen's
> guns tearing up the dust in their front, rear and sides. . . . [42]

When questioned, the captured scouts admitted that they were hunting for Brown. Friends then sent word to the abolitionist's camp, warning him that a posse was nearby. Brown reacted quickly. He rounded up his accomplices and rode into Prairie City, where nineteen townsmen volunteered to join him, bringing Brown's group to thirty in all.

Brown finally located Pate's posse near Black Jack ravine around 6:00 a.m. the following day. As Pate's scouts began to fire, more than half of Brown's volunteers fell back. Brown insisted upon going forward, even though he was now greatly outnumbered. For three hours, the two sides exchanged fire, much of which was poorly aimed. Even so, more and more of Pate's men abandoned their positions as the battle dragged on. Finally, one of Brown's sons, who had serious mental problems, rode into the fray, shouting to his father that the enemy was surrounded. Strangely enough, Pate accepted the announcement without question, and he and his men surrendered.

Eventually, federal troops from Fort Leavenworth arrived on the scene. Colonel Sumner freed Brown's twenty-three captives, including eight wounded men, and since he lacked a warrant for Brown's arrest—it had been lost—the abolitionist was not taken into custody. By this time, Sumner's troops were exhausted. Earlier that day they had prevented several hundred ruffians from attacking a group of abolitionists. Later, for the first time, the soldiers had been fired upon by Free Staters, who were trying to drive out a proslavery family, when they were found by Sumner's men. Clearly the situation was getting more dangerous each day, and the troops were stretched to their limit.

Believing that the soldiers were no longer a serious threat and emboldened by Brown's success, Lawrencians attacked nearby Franklin on June 4. Rumor had it that the cannon used to destroy the Free State Hotel was hidden away there. The Lawrencians were driven back by the very cannon they sought, which was loaded with nails because the town's defenders lacked cannonballs. After firing numerous rounds of ammunition, wounding a handful and killing one Franklin defender, the Free Staters withdrew.

On June 7, proslavery forces attacked Osawatomie in retaliation.

And so it went, one side attacking the other. No place was safe. Travelers on both sides of the slavery issue were stopped on the road and questioned about their political beliefs. Some were hanged when they gave the "wrong" answers. Others were rousted out of bed at night, dragged from their cabins, and hacked to death. Some farmers working in their fields were shot in the back by members of death squads, one of which was led by Charles Leonhardt, a Free Stater who was the main suspect in the shooting of Sheriff Jones. In addition to the mounting deaths, pillaging and looting became commonplace, and sometimes the attackers weren't as interested in their victims' political beliefs as they were in enriching themselves.

While various posses and militias had been fighting, Free Staters had continued to try to form their own government. But on July 4, 1856, federal troops, backed by several cannons, forced the Free State legislature to stop meeting.

At the same time, Free Staters were making pleas and giving speeches throughout the now very sympathetic North. One of the most popular representatives was Sara Robinson, whose husband was being held prisoner in a tent in Lecompte along with other Free State leaders. The most powerful speaker was James Lane, who was determined to do nothing less than raise an entire army to support the Free State movement. Not only did he inspire hundreds of men to become soldiers for a free Kansas; Lane's efforts led to the formation of the National Kansas Committee, which pledged more than $250,000 for the cause.

Proslavery forces were aghast at the change in the Free Staters. Envisioning thousands of weapons and more wild-eyed abolitionists flowing into the territory, ruffians immediately went to work to cut off every supply and travel route they could. Ferries on the Missouri were routinely checked for suspicious characters and roads leading to and from the ferries were patrolled by ruffian scouts. Any man, woman, or child who was thought to be a potential Free State supporter was turned back. But try as they might, proslavery forces couldn't possibly patrol the entire Missouri-Kansas border. Besides, there were other entries into the territory. Settlers and soldiers, including Lane's army, three hundred strong, simply took a longer route through Iowa and Nebraska.

In early August, Lane and his men reached the northern border of Kansas, where they were met by several Free State forces, including a group under John Brown. When Brown informed Lane that his men were desperately needed to help carry out several attacks, Lane decided to make a rapid march. The pace—150 miles in thirty hours— took its toll on men and horses, many of whom dropped from sheer exhaustion along the trail. In fact, the *only* member of the entire Army of the North to ride into Lawrence at the end of this march was Lane himself.

Free Staters immediately updated Lane. Buoyed by the knowledge that reinforcements, even though they were temporarily exhausted, were on their way, Lawrencians finalized their plans to attack Franklin again and to destroy two other proslavery strongholds that had cut off the Free Staters' supply lines.

On August 12, one day after Lane had arrived in Lawrence, a Free State force of about eighty men rode into Franklin. For approximately four hours they fired away without causing a single casualty among the defenders. Thoroughly frustrated, Lane's men pushed a wagon full of hay to the edge of the fort and set the hay on fire. Outmaneuvered, the defenders poured out of the fort and watched helplessly as Lane and his men gathered up weapons and an irreplaceable cannon for future battles. The fact that the Free Staters didn't have a single cannonball didn't bother them in the least. They planned to melt down the printing type that they had salvaged from the river after Lawrence's newspaper presses had been destroyed and use the scrap for ammunition.

Lane and his men, whose numbers had now soared to several hundred, then went on to attack Fort Saunders and Fort Titus. They managed to capture both without much difficulty and took a fair number of prisoners. Needless to say, Free Staters were jubilant.

Governor Shannon, on the other hand, was desperate. On August 17 he met first with Free Staters then with proslavery forces to try to end the fighting. Although Shannon did get both sides to agree to a truce, he was deeply alarmed by the change in the Free Staters' tactics. In a letter to General Pulsifer Smith, who was now in command at Fort Leavenworth, Shannon said, "We are threatened with utter extermination by a large force of free-state men. I have just returned from Lawrence, where I have been this day to [procure] the release of nineteen prisoners that were taken. I saw in that place at least 800 men who manifested a fixed purpose of destroying [Lecompton]."[43] The following day, Shannon resigned.

As Shannon headed east, he met briefly with his replacement, Governor John Geary. Geary's secretary, John Gihorn, summarized the meeting.

> A steamboat, bound down the river and directly from Kansas, came alongside [our boat]. Ex-governor Shannon was a passenger, who, upon learning the close proximity of Governor Geary, sought an immediate interview with him. The ex-governor was greatly agitated. He had fled in haste and terror from the territory, and seemed still to be laboring under an apprehension for his personal safety. His description of Kansas was suggestive of everything that is frightful and horrible. . . . The whole territory was in a state of insurrection, and a destructive civil war was devastating the country. Murder ran rampant, and the roads were everywhere strewn with the bodies of slaughtered men. No language can exaggerate the awful picture that was drawn.[44]

As Geary entered the territory, he saw proof of Shannon's statements everywhere.

Still, he was determined to bring about peace, and he had a three-fold plan that he hoped would end the violence. First, Geary ordered the proslavery courts back into action. Until his arrival, Free Staters had been arrested, refused bail, and denied trials, a foolproof means of keeping the enemy leaderless. Process the prisoners, Geary demanded, or he would replace the justices. Shortly after, more than five hundred men were released on bail, a dramatic action that reaped praise from the Free Staters. Next, the governor announced that he would support the current territorial legislature, which pleased proslavery forces. And third, Geary outlawed militias. To try to get the two sides to work together and defend the territory from Missourian invaders, Geary planned to form a territorial militia composed of Free Staters and proslavery supporters. This was an overly optimistic plan that failed to take into account the deep-seated hatred each side felt for the other. Besides, proslavery supporters weren't necessarily opposed to invaders from Missouri if they could help the supporters establish slavery in Kansas.

While Governor Geary was honing his plans for peace, David Atchison and the ruffians, reeling from recent setbacks and not too certain about the kind of support that they might get from Geary, sought a major military victory to pump life back into the proslavery movement. Atchison chose Lawrence as his target, and he rounded up three thousand men to destroy the town.

When Lawrencians received word that Atchison was on the move, they were stunned. Most of the townsmen were away, fighting proslavery forces in northern Kansas, leaving only John Brown and a handful of his followers to defend the town. Lawrencians immediately turned to Governor Geary for help.

On September 14, the first ruffians, led by Sheriff Jones, charged toward Lawrence. Townspeople, who had been told by John Brown to make every bullet count since they had few on hand, held their fire until the enemy was close. After Lawrencians let loose a few well-aimed rounds, Jones and his men turned and fled. Although the defenders were relieved, they knew that without help, they were doomed. Jones would simply return with more men. To the townspeople's great relief, federal troops arrived that night, and the governor himself the next day.

Geary approached the invaders first. Backed by well-armed soldiers, Geary told the militia, which was now illegal, to disband immediately. Next the governor met privately with proslavery leaders, warning them of dire consequences if they didn't put down their arms. Geary's secretary recalled:

Governor Geary at once summoned the officers together, and addressed them at length and with great feeling. He depicted in a forcible manner the improper position they occupied, and the untold horrors that would result from the consummation of their cruel designs: that if they persisted in their mad career, the entire Union would be involved in a civil war, and thousands and tens of thousands of innocent lives be sacrificed. To Atchison, he especially addressed himself, telling him that when he last saw him, he was acting as vice-president of the nation and president of the most dignified body of men in the world, the senate of the United States; but now with sorrow and pain he saw him leading on to a civil and disastrous war an army of men, with uncontrollable passions, and determined upon wholesale slaughter and destructions. [45]

When Geary had finished talking to proslavery forces, he turned his full attention to Free Staters. Eventually, both sides agreed to a truce. David Atchison and his men went back to Missouri, James Lane left the territory for reasons that are not clear, and John Brown, using his newly found fame and unshakable belief in his calling to end slavery, headed east to lay the groundwork for a massive slave revolt.

As Free Staters gained the upper hand around Lawrence, many proslavery supporters relocated in southeast Kansas. There they were greeted by antislavery agitator James Montgomery, a former minister, and his followers. This group called themselves the Jayhawkers, after a mythical bird, a Jayhawk, which was known for its big beak and fearless attacks. The Jayhawkers, under Montgomery's leadership, harassed the new settlers, stole their goods, and took their lives at will. The men were so bold that they actually conducted raids into Missouri, making them heroes in the Free Staters' eyes. These attacks, known as "Jayhawking," would continue well into 1858, when after proslavery forces massacred five free soilers Pottawatomie-style on the banks of the Marais des Cygnes River, both sides finally admitted that they had had enough bloodshed and once again promised to put their weapons away.

Harpers Ferry

Harpers Ferry

After spending almost two years in the East making plans for a massive slave revolt, John Brown returned to Kansas in 1858, where he accompanied James Montgomery's Jayhawkers for a short time. During one of the raids into Missouri, Brown and his men seized eleven slaves, whom he escorted along an Underground Railroad route that had been operating in Kansas since 1857. It was Brown's last visit to the territory.

For a while, Brown dropped out of sight. Then on a chilly, moonless night in October 1859, he and eighteen of his followers appeared outside Harpers Ferry, Virginia, where once again Brown was poised for an attack. He planned to seize weapons stored in a federal armory to free and arm as many slaves as he could for the first of many rebellions. After surveying the scene one last time, he ordered an assault. His followers cut telegraph lines, blocked exits from town, seized hostages, and took over federal property that contained several million dollars' worth of guns and ammunition.

But events didn't go exactly as Brown had planned. A doctor in Harpers Ferry ran for help after he managed to get past Brown's men, and before the abolitionists could free a single slave, local and federal troops rushed in. Ten of the raiders were killed or fatally wounded, including one of Brown's sons, Oliver, who had participated in the Pottawatomie Creek massacres in Kansas. The rest were captured by U.S. Marines under the temporary command of Colonel Robert E. Lee. John Brown was tried, found guilty of treason, and hanged on December 2, 1859.

During his trial, Brown's willingness to die for his cause—he rejected all rescue offers, even those from Montgomery and the Jayhawkers—earned the respect of many Northerners. And at the exact hour he was hanged, 11:00 a.m., church bells all over the North, including some bells in Kansas, rang out to show support, if not for Brown, then for the cause in which he believed.

Although the dream of a free state had been quashed when the Free State legislature had been disbanded, free soilers were encouraged the following spring. When Governor Geary resigned his post in May 1857, his replacement, Robert Walker, governor number four, had a long talk with Free State leaders. Walker pointed out that the Free Staters had no choice but to work with the proslavery government. Starting their own government had failed to win the day, he pointed out, and violent attacks had not fared any better. Besides, it was to the Free Staters' advantage to recognize the territorial government, imperfect as it was. If it wasn't accepted, then *all* laws and regulations, including those governing land claims, were null and void. Did the settlers really want to abandon their titles and start over? he wondered.

Charles Robinson and the others could make Kansas free, Governor Walker continued, through the ballot box. When Free Staters laughed aloud at this idea, the governor pointed out that Free Staters were now in the majority and that their numbers were growing as new settlers from the North moved into the territory. Given the richness and beauty of the land, he doubted that the flow of such emigrants would end any time soon. He also doubted that Southerners now saw Kansas as a site where slavery could flourish. Unlike most Southern states, where fields could be worked all year, cold Kansan winters meant long periods of idleness for slaves. Besides, unlike the typical crops grown in the South, cotton for example, growing and harvesting Kansan crops, especially wheat, did not require many field hands. So Free Staters couldn't fail, he said, especially if he posted soldiers near ballot boxes on election day to insure a fair election.

Free Staters met throughout the summer of 1857 to try to decide what to do. Eventually those who wanted to try the ballot box prevailed. They knew it was too late to put forth names for delegates to the constitutional convention. They would be elected in June. It wasn't practical to do so anyway, since boundaries of voting districts favored proslavery candidates. However, it was not too late to nominate candidates for the fall election for the territorial legislature. If Free Staters could win a majority of seats, leaders argued, the legislature could force

A Minister of the Devil?

A Minister of the Devil?

In December 1858, James Montgomery and his Jayhawkers rescued Benjamin Rice, a Free Stater who had been arrested for murder and was being held in a hotel in Fort Scott.

As Montgomery and his men charged toward the hotel, proslavery men scattered about the town grabbed their weapons. After firing away at Montgomery, John Little, a former officer of the law and proslavery advocate, leaned out of a shop window to see if he had hit the minister. One of Montgomery's men spotted him, took direct aim, and killed Little. His fiancée, Gene Campbell, wrote to Montgomery to express her feelings. Unfortunately, her anger and pain were not uncommon. Many lost loved ones while Kansas bled, and they, too, experienced similar emotions.

Fort Scott

January 4, 1859

Montgomery:

Listen to me. Today I heard that you said in a speech a few days ago that you were not sorry you had killed John Little. That he was not killed too soon. Can you before God say so? Oh, the anguish you have caused. He was one of the noblest men ever created, brave and true to his country and to his word. You can't prove that he ever injured an innocent person.

A few days more and we were to have been married, then go south to trouble you no more. But through your influence, he was killed. He was sent to another world without even time to pray or to say goodbye to his friends. But thanks to God, though you did kill his body, you can't touch his soul. No. No, it is in the spirit land. Now the cry of "the Osages [Indians] are coming!" can awaken him no more. He quietly sleeps in our little graveyard.

But remember this. I am a girl, but I can fire a pistol. And if ever the time comes, I will send some of you to the place where there is "weeping and gnashing of teeth". You, a minister of God? You mean a minister of the devil, and a very superior one too. I have no more to say to you and your imps. Please accept the sincere regards of your future repentance. [46]

———— ≡◊≡ ————

the delegates to put the constitution to a vote, giving Free Staters one last chance to make Kansas free.

That fall, proslavery constitutional delegates drew up a controversial document. Known as the Lecompton Constitution, one section guaranteed that slaves in the territory and their children, and their children's children, and so on, would remain property. This section was meant to appease slaveholders in Kansas and was considered so important that it would not be put to a vote. However, another clause that permitted the *expansion* of slavery, that is, bringing in more slaves, was to be put before Kansans for approval.

Irate Free Staters refused to cast ballots. To do so was a farce! they shouted. Even if we vote this down, we shall still be saddled with slavery. We want a voice on the entire document, they insisted, and a chance to vote out *all* slavery! Delegates wouldn't budge, and when proslavery supporters finished voting, the section permitting the expansion of slavery passed, 6,226 to 569. But the fight wasn't over.

Free Staters had won a majority in the territorial legislature in the fall, and they took office in January 1858. Immediately the legislature forced the delegates to put the Lecompton Constitution before the people later that month. Proslavery forces considered the issue settled, so now they refused to go to the polls. As a result, the constitution, and slavery, limited or otherwise, was rejected, 10,226 to 162.

Inexplicably, President James Buchanan, who had been in office for ten months, urged Congress to admit Kansas to the Union under this constitution anyway. The Senate agreed to do so, despite heroic efforts on the part of Stephen A. Douglas to reject the document. He insisted that Congress was honor-bound to accept the will of the people—what popular sovereignty was all about—even if its members didn't like the decision Kansans had made. The House of Representatives agreed with Douglas, and refused to accept the constitution.

Still trying to make Kansas into a slave state, members from the Senate and the House met to try to work out a compromise. The result was the English bill, which offered Kansans over five million acres beyond their original request if settlers would reconsider their decision and ratify the Lecompton Constitution. Kansans rejected this bribe by a vote of 11,300 to 1,788.

Another constitutional convention was called in Wyandotte in July. This time, delegates drafted a document that outlawed slavery. Period. The majority of the delegates were antislavery, and proslavery forces, realizing that they couldn't win, had given up. In October 1858, Kansans passed what is now known as the Wyandotte Constitution, which is still in effect, 10,241 to 5,530. Once again, Kansas applied for statehood.

Congressmen fought over the territory's admission to the Union for almost a year. Not only were Southerners deeply upset over losing Kansas for their side, they were firmly resolved on blocking the admission of any free states in order to prevent the Northern voting block from becoming more powerful. Besides, as long as Kansas was still a territory, slavery was permitted there. As a result, Kansas was not admitted to the Union until January 29, 1861, after South Carolina had seceded from the Union and other Southern states were planning to do likewise.

Kansans rejoiced once statehood had been achieved, for the long, difficult struggle was finally over. But their joy was tempered. On the horizon loomed an even greater struggle that would involve many Kansans, a struggle more bloody than Bleeding Kansas had been and more difficult than anyone could have imagined at the time—the Civil War.

Afterword

On December 20, 1860, South Carolina seceded from the Union. South Carolinians encouraged other slave states to do likewise, and Alabama, Florida, Georgia, Louisiana, and Mississippi quickly agreed. They formed the Confederate States of America on February 4, 1861. Squabbles broke out between Union and Confederate forces over who owned what, and on April 12 when Union soldiers refused to abandon Fort Sumter near Charleston, South Carolina, the first shots of the Civil War were fired. Three days later, President Abraham Lincoln issued a nationwide call for troops, making it perfectly clear that he intended to use force to restore the Union. Now the remaining slave states, Arkansas, Delaware, Kentucky, Maryland, Missouri, North Carolina, Tennessee, Texas, and Virginia had to decide whether they would join their sister states or take up arms against them.

Many Missourians, especially slaveholders, favored secession. But after some long, bitter debates, the state's leaders decided to remain in the Union. Some Missourians would not accept this decision, and they took to the hills to wage a guerrilla war.

The goals of these guerrillas were to seize goods for the Confederate cause, cut Union supply lines, and wear down the enemy, which included their neighbors in Kansas. As a result, a border war sprang up between the old Jayhawkers, now the 7th Kansas Volunteer Cavalry Regiment under the leadership of Charles Jennison, and the guerrillas whom Kansans called "bushwackers." One of the most famous guerrillas was William Quantrill, whose followers included Coleman and Jim Younger and their cousins, Frank and Jesse James, who would later become some of America's most famous outlaws.

The attacks on both sides were daring and ruthless, and were often fought more to enrich the raiders than to help their side. In fact, the assaults actually hurt their cause. Jennison's forays were so brutal that he drove many Missourians into the arms of the Confederacy. As a result, Union leaders eventually removed him from the scene. Quantrill's assaults were even more cruel, if that was possible. He and his followers, known as "Quantrill's raiders," sacked Lawrence on August 21,1863, gunning down 150 men in cold blood in front of their wives and children and setting the town on fire. High on the wanted list of every Kansan after that, Quantrill was also forced to leave the area to avoid capture.

To prevent more raids on Kansans, Union General Thomas Ewing ordered the evacuation of four western counties in Missouri where citizens were known to shelter the guerrillas. To make sure that the people didn't return, soldiers burned their homes to the ground.

Jayhawkers and bushwackers may have dominated the news in Kansas, especially in the beginning of the war, but the Civil War in Kansas was a lot more than a border war. Although only one major battle, the battle of Mine Creek in 1864, was fought in the state, more than twenty thousand Kansans volunteered for service in the Union Army, fighting in numerous battles far from home.

Also, the war created a great demand for foodstuffs. Even though they were terribly shorthanded, Kansans who remained at home somehow managed to produce, on average, 200,000 bushels of wheat and six million bushels of corn each year, the majority of which went to the Union army. In addition, Kansans soon learned that their lush

During the Civil War, Kansans produced approximately 200,000 bushels of wheat each year. Courtesy of the Kansas State Historical Society, Topeka, Kansas

200,000 bushels of wheat

grasslands were ideal sites for raising horses, mules, and beef cattle, all of which the Union army eagerly sought. So, on one hand, the war brought death and hardship to soldiers and their families, and on the other hand, economic prosperity.

The war also changed the lives of some of the characters involved in Bleeding Kansas, including antislavery advocates James Lane, Hannah Ropes and Charles and Sara Robinson; proslavery supporters such as David Atchison and Sheriff Samuel Jones; and the author of the Kansas-Nebraska bill, Stephen A. Douglas.

James Lane, who had been elected senator when Kansas was admitted as a state, had barely reached Washington, D.C., when the war broke out. He found a city in turmoil, for citizens and legislators alike feared an invasion from the Confederacy at any moment. Eager for action, Lane rounded up every Kansan male in the capital, fifty in all, and established a group of volunteers known as the Frontier Guard. He then offered his services to the War Department. On April 18, 1861, Lane and his men were assigned to the White House to protect the president. Soldiers poured into the capital in the following days and reinforced the city's defenses. The Frontier Guard was then dismissed.

Lane returned to Kansas whenever possible during his term in office. He helped form two Kansas volunteer regiments, both of which fought against Confederate forces in western Missouri. He even led several raids into that state where he helped free a number of slaves.

In 1865, Lane was reelected to the Senate. After Lincoln's assassination in April, Lane abandoned the Radical Republicans, a group of representatives and senators, including Charles Sumner, who wanted to punish the South as severely as possible when the war was over. Lane backed President Andrew Johnson and his more lenient program for reuniting the country, hoping that by doing so, Lane would continue to receive the same privileges he had enjoyed under President Lincoln. This included the right to appoint many of his friends to government offices. However, his turnabout infuriated Kansans, and they heaped criticism upon him. By this time, Lane was physically and mentally exhausted. Unable to face *any* insults and unable to present his case to the voters, he became despondent. Lane shot himself on July 1, 1866. He died ten days later.

Hannah Ropes was also involved in the Civil War. Fearing the outbreak of violence in the spring of 1856, Hannah had returned to Massachusetts where she wrote *Six Months in Kansas, by a Lady.* When the war broke out and the federal government announced that it would hire women to care for wounded soldiers, a first in American history, Hannah applied for a position. She served as the head of the nurses in the Union Hotel Hospital in Washington, one of many buildings put to use by the army. In 1863, she contracted typhoid fever at work. She died shortly after.

Dr. Charles and Sara Robinson remained in Kansas during the war. Dr. Robinson served as the state's first governor from 1861 to1863, and one of his most important tasks was to recruit soldiers for the Union army. Like many former Free Staters, he joined the Republican party. Due to a scandal about the sale of some state bonds, he was defeated in the next election.

Robinson and James Lane sparred throughout the war for political influence in Kansas. Eventually Lane succeeded in driving the governor from the Republican party, and Robinson became a political maverick, running as an Independent Reform candidate in one election, a National Labor Greenback in another. Robinson served in the state legislature from 1874 to1878.

After Sara Robinson published *Kansas—Its Interior and Exterior Life*, in 1856, she became one of the best-known women in the territory. As the governor's wife, she continued to occupy a place in the spotlight, speaking out on issues whenever she felt a need to do so.

The Robinsons spent their last years on a farm three miles north of Lawrence, where Charles died in 1894. They were enthusiastic supporters of the University of Kansas, and they donated the land upon which the first classrooms were built. When Sara died in 1911, the entire Robinson estate was given to the school.

David Atchison's life also changed during the war. When Missouri failed to secede and all males of fighting age in his home state were expected to volunteer for the Union army, Atchison moved to Texas, which became part of the Confederacy. He returned to Missouri after the Union was restored. However, few secessionists played a major role in politics after the war, and Atchison was no exception. He spent his last years on a farm near Columbia, where he died in 1886.

Sheriff Samuel Jones faded from the history books after Kansas became a state. Historians do know that he stayed in Kansas, where he joined the Republican party, which he had once attacked with great vigor, when Southern Democrats backed secession. Like many fellow proslavery supporters in Kansas, Jones, thoroughly sick of bloodshed and rebel governments, called secessionists "treasonous villains."

And finally, Stephen A. Douglas, who was so instrumental in the struggle over Kansas, also found his life forever changed, first by the results of his Kansas-Nebraska Act, and then by the war itself. Although Douglas won reelection to his senate seat in 1858—he ran against

Abraham Lincoln—many Northern Democrats were no longer supportive of the senator's popular sovereignty strategy, which they blamed for the bloodshed in Kansas. As a result, fellow Democrats began to strip Douglas of his power, and they removed him from the chairmanship of the Committee on Territories.

Undeterred, Douglas ran for president of the United States in 1860. This time he lost to Lincoln.

After shots were fired at Fort Sumter, President Lincoln asked Douglas to speak to the people who had voted for him in the last election to convince them that the Union had to be kept together at all costs. Douglas quickly agreed to do so. In the following weeks, he worked to the point of exhaustion. Weakened and heartsick at the very thought of civil war, Douglas became ill in late April. He died from typhoid fever on June 3, 1861.

Notes

1. Eric Corder, *Prelude to Civil War: Kansas-Missouri, 1854-61* (New York: Crowell-Collier Press, 1970), p. 78.

2. Thomas Goodrich, *War to the Knife: Bleeding Kansas, 1854-1861* (Mechanicsburg, Penn., 1998), pp. 126, 127.

3. Goodrich, *War to the Knife*, p. 128.

4. Goodrich, *War to the Knife*, p. 129.

5. Corder, *Prelude to Civil War*, p. 14.

6. Corder, *Prelude to Civil War*, p. 15.

7. Goodrich, *War to the Knife*, p. 12.

8. Miriam Davis Colt, *Went to Kansas: Being a Thrilling Account of an Ill-fated Expedition to that Fairy Land, and Its Sad Results* (Watertown: L. Ingalls & Co., 1862, Internet Public Library, www.ipl.org), Chapter 5, p. 3.

9. Goodrich, *War to the Knife*, p. 10.

10. Goodrich, *War to the Knife*, p. 61.

11. Hannah Anderson Ropes, *Six Months in Kansas, by a Lady* (Boston: John P. Jewett and Company, 1856), pp. 12, 13, 20, 22, 31, 33, 34, 44.

12. Goodrich, *War to the Knife*, p. 32.

13. Corder, *Prelude to Civil War*, p. 25.

14. Corder, *Prelude to Civil War*, p. 27.

15. Corder, *Prelude to Civil War*, p. 37.

16. Sara T.D. Robinson, *Kansas—Its Interior and Exterior Life* (Boston: Crosby, Nichols and Company, 1856, Internet Public Library, www.ipl.org), Chapter 6, pp. 6, 7.

17. Robinson, *Kansas—Its Interior and Exterior Life*, Chapter 6, p. 6; Chapter 8, pp. 2, 3.

18. Robinson, *Kansas—Its Interior and Exterior Life*, Chapter 9, p. 2.

19. Goodrich, *War to the Knife*, p. 76.

20. Corder, *Prelude to Civil War*, p. 45.

21. Ropes, *Six Months in Kansas*, p. 119.

22. Ropes, *Six Months in Kansas*, p.121.

23. Robinson, *Kansas—Its Interior and Exterior Life*, Chapter 9, p. 5.

24. Robinson, *Kansas—Its Interior and Exterior Life*, Chapter 9, p. 7.

25. Ropes, *Six Months in Kansas*, pp. 120, 121, 122.

26. Corder, *Prelude to Civil War*, p. 47.

27. Corder, *Prelude to Civil War*, p. 54.

28. Robinson, *Kansas—Its Interior and Exterior Life*, Chapter 11, p. 12.

29. Robinson, *Kansas—Its Interior and Exterior Life*, Chapter 12, p. 5.

30. Goodrich, *War to the Knife*, p. 90.

31. Ropes, *Six Months in Kansas*, pp. 209, 210, 211.

32. Robinson, *Kansas—Its Interior and Exterior Life*, Chapter 13, p. 3.

33. Robinson, *Kansas—Its Interior and Exterior Life*, Chapter 12, pp. 10, 11.

34. William C. Cutler, *History of the State of Kansas* (Chicago: A T. Andreas, 1883, Internet Public Library, www.ipl.org), Part 29, p. 2.

35. Goodrich, *War to the Knife*, pp. 110, 111.

36. John H. Gihon, *Geary and Kansas—Governor Geary's Administration in Kansas With Complete History of the Territory Until June 1857* (Philadelphia: Charles C. Rhodes, 1857, Internet Public Library, www.ipl.org), Chapter 13, p. 1.

37. Cutler, *History of the State of Kansas*, Part 33, p. 3.

38. Charles Sumner, "On the Crime Against Kansas" (www.iath. virginia.edu/seminar/unit 4/sumner.html), pp. 2, 3, 4.

39. Goodrich, *War to the Knife*, p. 120.

40. Cutler, *History of the State of Kansas*, Part 33, p. 3.

41. Robinson, *Kansas—Its Interior and Exterior Life*, Chapter 16, p. 14.

42. Goodrich, *War to the Knife*, p. 132.

43. Corder, *Prelude to Civil War*, p. 98.

44. Gihon, *Geary and Kansas*, Chapter 17, p. 2.

45. Gihon, *Geary and Kansas*, Chapter 24, p. 4.

46. Fort Scott National Historic Site (www.nps.gov/fosc/bleeding.html), "Bleeding Kansas," page 3.

Bibliography

Brumgardt, John R., *Civil War Nurse: The Diary and Letters of Hannah Ropes.* Knoxville: University of Tennessee Press, 1980.

Castel, Albert. *A Frontier State at War: Kansas, 1861-1865.* Ithaca, N. Y.: Cornell University Press, 1958.

_____. *Civil War Kansas: Reaping the Whirlwind.* Lawrence: University Press of Kansas, 1997.

Colt, Miriam Davis. *Went to Kansas: Being a Thrilling Account of an Ill-fated Expedition to that Fairy Land, and Its Sad Results.* Watertown: L. Ingalls & Co., 1862. (Internet Public Library, www.ipl.org).

Corder, Eric. *Prelude to Civil War: Kansas-Missouri, 1854-61.* New York: Crowell—Collier Press, 1970.

Cutler, William C. *History of the State of Kansas.* Chicago: A.T. Andreas, 1883. (Internet Public Library, www.ipl.org).

Davis, Kenneth S. *Kansas: A Bicentennial History.* New York: W.W. Norton & Company, Inc., 1976.

Gihon, John H. *Geary and Kansas—Governor Geary's Administration in Kansas With Complete History of the Territory Until June 1857.* Philadelphia: Charles C. Rhodes, 1857. (Internet Public Library, www.ipl.org).

Goodrich, Thomas. *War to the Knife: Bleeding Kansas, 1854-1861.* Mechanicsburg, Penn.: Stackpole Books, 1998.

Oates, Stephen B. *To Purge This Land with Blood: A Biography of John Brown.* New York: Harper & Row, Publishers, 1970.

Renehan, Edward J., Jr. *The Secret Six: The True Tale of the Men Who Conspired with John Brown.* Columbia: University of South Carolina Press, 1997.

Richmond, Robert W. *Kansas: A Pictorial History.* Lawrence: University of Kansas Press, 1992.

Robinson, Sara T.D. *Kansas—Its Interior and Exterior Life.* Boston: Crosby, Nichols and Company, 1856. (Internet Public Library, www.ipl.org).

Ropes, Hannah Anderson. *Six Months in Kansas, by a Lady.* Boston: John P. Jewett and Company, 1856.

For More Information

For more information about events in Bleeding Kansas, check out the Kansas Museum of History's web site (http://www.kshs.org). This site provides pictures of and information about: the Shawnee Mission; the first territorial capitol; the Adair cabin, where John Brown often stayed; Constitution Hall; the Marais des Cygnes massacre; the Goodnow house, which was the home of one of the first free-soil settlers in the territory; and the Mine Creek battlefield, where the only major Civil War battle was fought in Kansas. This site also provides access to a wealth of firsthand accounts, many of which are suitable for young adult readers. Another source about Bleeding Kansas is a book by James P. Barry, *Bloody Kansas, 1854-65: Guerrilla Warfare Delays Peaceful American Settlement* (New York: Franklin Watts, 1972).

To learn more about the history and the state of Kansas, read Nancy Robinson Masters's book, *Kansas* (New York: Children's Press, 1999) or explore the Kansas Information Network (www.state.ks.us). You might also want to look at *Kansas—A Pictorial History* by Robert W. Richmond (Lawrence: University Press of Kansas, 1992).

And finally, to learn more about some of the people involved in Bleeding Kansas check out: *Fiery Vision: The Life and Death of John Brown* (New York: Scholastic, 1997) by Clinton Cox; *John Brown, A Cry for Freedom* (New York: Crowell, 1980) by Lorenz Graham; and *The Little Giant: Stephen A. Douglas* (New York: Messner, 1964) by Jeannette Nolan.

Acknowledgments

The author wishes to thank the staff of the Kansas State Historical Society in Topeka for its invaluable assistance. The society's archives house a wealth of reference materials as well as a vast array of photos, all of which were readily—and cheerfully— made available.

Index

Page numbers are given in bold for individual portraits.